Eight Habits of Healthy, Happy Kids

TYNDALE
REFRESH™

Think Well. Live Well. Be Well.

8

HABITS OF

Healthy, Happy Kids

SECRETS TO RAISING CHILDREN WHO THRIVE

RHONDA SPENCER-HWANG, DrPH, MPH

Visit Tyndale online at tyndale.com.

Tyndale and Tyndale's quill logo are registered trademarks of Tyndale House Ministries. *Tyndale Refresh* and the Tyndale Refresh logo are trademarks of Tyndale House Ministries. Tyndale Refresh is a nonfiction imprint of Tyndale House Publishers, Carol Stream, Illinois.

Eight Habits of Healthy, Happy Kids: Secrets to Raising Children Who Thrive

Adapted from *Raising Resilient Kids*, published in 2021 under ISBN 978-1-4964-4508-7.

Cover designed by Julie Chen

Scripture quotations are taken from the *Holy Bible*, New Living Translation, copyright © 1996, 2004, 2015 by Tyndale House Foundation. Used by permission of Tyndale House Publishers, Carol Stream, Illinois 60188. All rights reserved.

For information about special discounts for bulk purchases, please contact Tyndale House Publishers at csresponse@tyndale.com, or call 1-855-277-9400.

Library of Congress Cataloging-in-Publication Data

A catalog record for this book is available from the Library of Congress.

ISBN 978-1-4964-7230-4

Printed in the United States of America

29	28	27	26	25	24	23
7	6	5	4	3	2	1

Contents

A Note Before
You Begin

EIGHT HABITS OF HEALTHY, HAPPY KIDS introduces you to eight healthy habits that centenarians (people one hundred years or older) have practiced since childhood that may improve your family's overall health as well. Before making major changes to health practices such as diet and exercise, however, be sure to consult with your physician.

One-Hundred-Year-Old Wisdom

*Direct your children onto the right
path, and when they are older,
they will not leave it.*

PROVERBS 22:6

ON A MILD CALIFORNIA WINTER'S DAY a few years
ago, I sat on the patio watching my youngest child,
one-year-old Julia, babbling away in the sandbox.
Her brother and sister were already at school, and
I had no classes to teach that day. I didn't have
to rush off to a meeting, answer an email, give a
health presentation, drive car pool, or settle sibling disputes. I relished this unhurried moment
of calm.

Yet I felt uneasy. I knew something was not
right, and I was headed for trouble. I was teaching
public health at a university, but privately my kids
and I were devouring junk food. I was teaching the

importance of physical exercise and movement but spent most of my time sitting at my desk working while my kids sat in front of the TV. I was dedicated to my church, but my family and I were missing more services than we attended. I had lost my direction—and worse, I was setting up my kids to follow the same rocky path.

Watching Julia dig her way to China with her plastic shovel, I thought about how far our family had drifted from a healthy lifestyle. Like so many other parents, I was overwhelmed by the endless bombardment of daily challenges, accompanied by heaping doses of exhausting stress. I found myself making one subconscious decision after another.

Fast food just this once. I'm too tired to cook.
A marathon of TV for the kids just for today.
It's sure to settle them down.
Skipping church just this week. We've got so much to do.

Such days had turned into months and months into years, until these continual "exceptions" to the rule had *become* the rule—and soon characterized our daily lives. Making matters worse, my husband and I were paying for those unsettling selections not only with our own personal health, but with our kids' health as well.

Ironically, I live and work in Loma Linda, California, a community known worldwide for the health, extraordinary resilience, and longevity of its citizens. Often referred to as a Blue Zone, Loma Linda is one of only five regions in the world—and the only one in North America—with clusters of centenarians, men and women who have reached a vibrant one hundred years of age.[1]

Since many studies have shown that our habits and experiences in childhood lay the foundation for our health as adults, I suspected that these senior citizens had much to teach today's parents about how to raise healthy, happy kids. I interviewed as many of them as I could.[2]

It turns out, there were eight habits that virtually all of the centenarians had practiced in their childhoods and throughout the course of their lives. These habits helped build resilience and likely provided protection from all the hardships and adversity the centenarians faced, including the 1918 Spanish flu pandemic and many other outbreaks that often resulted in the death of family members, abuse, neglect, economic uncertainty during the Great Depression, and so many other adverse childhood experiences (ACEs) and stress-ors. Furthermore, I believe that if developed early, these same habits will result in both immediate and long-term physical and mental benefits for our kids (and us as well!).

This has been a life-changing journey for me, and I believe it can be life-changing for you too. Let's get started.

Active Movement and Outdoor Engagement

*In every walk with Nature, one
receives far more than he seeks.*

JOHN MUIR

As I TALKED WITH CENTENARIANS, one thing
became immediately clear—their early-twentieth-
century childhoods were far different from the
technology-driven, sedentary, and isolated childhoods that today's children typically experience.

Through their hundred-year-old eyes, I caught
a glimpse of a much quieter and more connected
time. They had been raised in slower-paced, do-it-
yourself (DIY) communities—with an emphasis
on community. Families didn't go it alone—they
depended on one another. They also relied on
much simpler forms of technology to communi-
cate and get things done.

While today's technologies are supposed to make life easier, they tend to lead to increasingly hectic lives, demanding even more of our professional and personal time. Meanwhile, children spend most of their time indoors, glued to computers or watching TV, rather than playing outside in nature or with their friends.

In fact, a survey by the National Trust found that children today spend half the time their parents did playing outdoors.[1] According to the Child Mind Institute, children spend on average just four to seven minutes a day in unstructured play outside![2] More alarming, they spend an average of seven hours per day sitting and staring at electronic screens, moving nothing but the distal digits of their fingers. Author Richard Louv coined the term *nature-deficit disorder* to describe this phenomenon.[3]

In contrast, most of the centenarians had been raised in farming families who maintained an active outdoor lifestyle immersed in physical activity from dawn to dusk, doing chores, caring for younger siblings, and helping their families garden and raise livestock. Their active lifestyles helped both girls and boys develop strong bones and muscles, avoid depression, and increase their energy levels, confidence, and life skills.

"I loved to work on the farm," said one-hundred-year-old Lidia Reichel, "[whether digging] in the soil or getting the cows and milking them. We used to do everything around the house. It's not like these days—you go to the supermarket and buy food. . . . As soon as we learned how to walk and talk, we had to work. My mom would dig into the soil and plant, and I'd help her."

While you don't have to buy a farm or force your kids to plant fields and harvest crops, if you want your kids to be happier and healthier, take a lesson from the centenarians and get your kids moving!

MODERN TIMES CALL FOR MODERN METHODS

Trying to replicate the childhoods of current centenarians presents one small problem. The very fact that they are centenarians means that they experienced childhood nearly a century ago! Think about how much our world has changed in the last hundred years. For the centenarians, even going to the bathroom as children meant donning coats (if it was winter) and heading outdoors to use the family's outhouse.

Today most people no longer live on farms, many have small yards or no yards at all, both parents may work full-time jobs, and children receive much more demanding homework and have longer school days than the centenarians ever did. Add to that the many structured activities for kids, from organized sports to other extracurricular activities, and the challenge grows greater. Most children work indoors from sunup to sundown, with little time or opportunity to get outdoors.

We lack the freedom the centenarians once had to roam the countryside without parental supervision, knowing they'd more than likely come home safe and sound for supper. So getting your children out the door—spending time together outside when you have work to do yourself—might seem like quite the mountain to climb.

Here's the good news: Just because the world has changed does not mean you can't engage with nature. If you commit to getting outdoors and being active, you'll find ways to make it happen.

To get started, do as the centenarians did: Keep it simple. If you make too many changes right from the start, you'll be more likely to give up.

Instead, take incremental steps. With time, you'll find that by beginning with just a few small adjustments to your daily life, you can achieve profound lifestyle changes.

Step 1: Develop your outdoor purpose

The centenarians I spoke with spent active time outdoors each day when they were children, but they didn't need to be encouraged; it was their way of life.

One-hundred-year-old Evelyn Reickman remembers going outdoors each day to take care of her family's cattle on their hundred acres. "There was no fencing on the farm, so it was a big job," she recalls. Likewise, 101-year-old Salma Mohr would walk barefoot into town every morning before breakfast to fetch milk in a coffee can for her family—ten children in all. Without her efforts, there would have been no milk for the day. Beyond outdoor work, they found trees to climb, ponds to fish, and woods to explore.

Instead of thinking only of exercises you can do indoors, start thinking of things you need or want to do that require physical activity outdoors. Start with fifteen minutes a day. Walk around the block to mail that letter. If you have a yard, go outside and clean it up, plant something, weed something, do something! If all you and your kids have is a balcony, rotate time out there with them. One child could repot plants with you, another might deadhead the flowers, and yet another could do homework outdoors. Just get them outside doing something!

Try getting a dog, caring for a farm animal, or planting a garden. Gardening, for instance, provides an immediate purpose for getting outdoors each day. Consider planting a garden with a theme—an herb garden, an aromatic garden, or a garden of flowers that bloom only at night. Try making a fairy garden by building miniature houses from twigs, bits of bark, pine cones, leaves, and whatever else you can find. If you don't have a yard, try a container garden set on a patio, inquire about local community gardens, or see if you can start a garden at your kids' school.

If you have the space, consider caring for livestock or outdoor pets such as chickens or rabbits. Even if you live in the city, having your own vegetable garden or some simple livestock—like chickens—will put your family on the path toward becoming more self-sustaining, which can be especially important during troubling times (like economic depressions or global virus outbreaks). You can check your local city laws to see what types of animals are allowed and how many.

Will your kids squawk at first about going outside? Will they try it once and think they've made sufficient sacrifice? Probably. Don't let their resistance defeat you. Be firm about your commitment to getting outdoors. The younger your children, the easier it will be to acclimate them to playing outside. Older children, such as my nine-year-old daughter, may resist more. Most need encouragement. Make it clear that staying indoors is not an option. Take away electronics if you have to.

Once you do get outside, don't rush. During their early childhoods, the centenarians I spoke with escaped the frenetic or competitive sports-like pace of modern life. The meditative quality of their peaceful outdoor time lowered their blood pressure, calmed their nerves, and helped them relax.

No matter where you live, there's a door to the outdoors. Open it.

Ninety-nine-year-old June Ohashi recalled the

tremendous challenge she faced as a teenager because of her Japanese heritage. World War II had broken out, and there was often hostility toward Japanese living in America. June had to decide whether to remain where she was living and attending school or return home. She remembers heading outdoors to a serene nature area and walking all around to help gain clarity on the decision she had to make.

During the recent COVID-19 pandemic, spending time outdoors and away from people worked wonders in reducing household tension. No matter where you live, there's a door to the outdoors. Open it. You never know what you might find. Some kids have even found a purpose for getting active in nature that's tied with a positive social benefit. A smart nine-year-old boy named Robbie Bond, a Hawaiian native, grew up on Oahu and always had a passion for being physically active outdoors. When he heard that the White House was reviewing national monuments and parks, intending to downsize or eliminate twenty-seven of them, Robbie convinced his family to visit as many of these monuments as possible over a six-month period. He not only got himself and his family moving, Robbie started a national movement when he became founder of Kids Speak for Parks, the nonprofit he launched in July 2017.[4]

Step 2: Use your feet for travel

How many times have you found yourself getting in the car to drive less than a mile to visit someone or pick up something at the store that you could easily have carried back home? With car accidents most likely to happen within five miles of your home, you quite literally risk your life to drive less than a mile! Instead of turning the key in the ignition, consider simply putting one foot in front of the other—there's a reason we were created to be bipedal. Our feet get us places.

One-hundred-year-old Evelyn Reickman didn't make a fuss about walking places as a child. Her longest journey each week was a whopping six-mile walk with her family to church and another six miles home. Without ready access to cars, getting around to nearby neighbors, schools, places of worship, and most other activities meant walking many miles—often for two to three hours a day. While walking that much today may seem unrealistic, perhaps you can promote living more like the centenarians by walking your children to school or enjoying a walking adventure to the store or library. If you can sit for an hour, you can walk for an hour. Sitting for an hour will drain you of your energy, while walking for an hour will increase it. Try it for a week and see how much better you feel!

Try not to let the rain or snow deter you. Encourage your children to get outdoors in different types of weather—with appropriate clothing. If they balk—and they will—acknowledge the unpleasant conditions but tell them you're going out anyway. Make the weather challenge a part of your adventure. If it's hot, be sure you've got plenty of water and sunscreen. Then splash in a pool or get out the garden hose. If it's raining, feel the drops fall on your face and watch them bounce in the puddles. Of course, don't go out if there's any thunder or lightning—lightning is nothing to play with. But a cloudy day, a nip in the air, or a bit of rain or snow falling from the sky can turn an ordinary day into an extraordinary one.

Need some additional inspiration? Consider 101-year-old Dr. Ellsworth Wareham. The climate in Alberta, Canada, where young Ellsworth grew up, could range from bitterly cold temperatures and heavy snowfall in the winter to highs in the nineties in the summer and everything in between. Even on the coldest days, Ellsworth would get up each morning around 4 a.m. to fetch the cows and milk them by hand before eating breakfast and heading off to school. In fact, most of the centenarians stayed outdoors throughout the day in every season, experiencing all kinds of weather. Many indigenous people and peasant farmers continue to live this way in other parts of the world— entire families living in mud homes no bigger than most of our bedrooms. It takes nothing short of a cyclone to keep them indoors. Houses are for eating and sleeping in much of the world; the outdoors is for living. So don't let weather keep you locked up indoors.

Step 3: Simplify your requirements for getting outdoors

The centenarians lived a simpler lifestyle than most of us today. With limited financial income, they connected with the outdoors organically, taking a hands-on, do-it-yourself approach to getting things done. In addition to making his own kites as a child, 105-year-old Dr. Robert Boltan helped his father make sleds to enjoy the snow.

Like the centenarians, wear clothing that encourages you and your children to be active outdoors. In warm weather, ditch the heels, sandals, or flip-flops and opt for sturdy tennis shoes. If girls prefer dresses, be sure they wear shorts or leggings underneath so they can climb and run. The same goes for you—get out of your suit and dress shoes and replace them with walking shoes and activewear.

Most of the centenarians I spoke with grew up extremely poor, so they made do with what they had on hand. Rather than shop at Eddie Bauer before an outing, they simply hiked—knowing the terrain and not putting themselves into risky situations, of course. They didn't buy tents that cost a week's wages; they camped under the stars or made shelters of their own. They often used what they had around them and stayed close to their homes.

Houses are for eating and sleeping in much of the world; the outdoors is for living.

Have you ever thought about untapped opportunities that might be available in your own community? Sometimes we have resources we aren't aware of. Many local communities offer outdoor adventures in zoos, public gardens, forest preserves, and even museums. You might call ahead of time to ask if they have any hidden attractions, tours, or just plain advice to help make your trip even more fun. By seeking insider tips prior to a museum visit in San Francisco, my family and I ended up taking a semiprivate and memorable outdoor tour of a flower field surrounding a whale bone graveyard.

The centenarians didn't routinely take vacations, but if those are a treasured part of your family's life, consider heading to local or distant campgrounds to spend time in the "wild." The simpler the camping experience, the better. You don't need a fancy recreational vehicle or elaborate camping gear. A modest tent and simple camp stove will help you temporarily leave modern times behind while you enjoy nature.

Another option: Visit a national park. Make your plans well in advance and reserve a camping space online. Read books on outdoor survival skills that teach you how to live with nature while in it—not how to replicate indoor living or "glamping." Learn to make and cook simple meals over an open fire, to fish, and perhaps even to forage for edible foods (though be cautious). Pack food in tight containers so you don't attract animals, and don't leave your toothbrush out overnight—a lesson I learned when a raccoon used mine as his personal body comb and paw cleaner!

If you live in a cold climate, winter may seem a challenging time to get outdoors, but take advantage of sunny, warmer winter days to enjoy places and activities that are rare (or nonexistent) in warmer climates: outdoor ice-skating rinks, sledding hills, and ice-carving festivals. Snow brings out the kid in all of us, so join in with your children as they build snowmen or snow forts. The Scandinavians even have a saying: "There's no such thing as bad weather, only bad clothing"!

READY, SET, GO!

Whatever you choose to do to make outdoor living a part of your natural life, start small. Don't try to conquer Mother Nature your first week stepping out. Try varied activities to discover what works best for you and your family, and where you find your greatest joy. When mishaps occur—and they will—address them and carry on. Don't let skinned knees, bee stings, or mosquitoes keep you from living your life. You belong in nature as much as any other creature.

Be prepared for protests from your kids, but also be prepared to change your life for the better once you put the keystone principles into practice.

Here are a few ways to include active movement and nature engagement in your daily life:

- Park your car on the distant edge of parking lots during the day so you can walk a bit farther (avoid doing so at night if it might be dangerous). This tip comes from martial arts master Bruce Lee, who never parked near his destination. Sometimes my kids and I use the parking lot voyage to pretend we are jungle animals making our way to the store. We've even had teenagers join us!

- Get a jump rope, Hula-Hoop, and resistance stretch bands, and engage your family in competitions on the lawn. Who can jump rope the longest or has the funniest style on the Hula-Hoop? You'll have fun and get in shape. I can almost assure you of laughter and family bonding.

- Get a Fitbit (available for both kids and adults) that will let you know when you need to move. Before I adopted the lifestyle of the centenarians, I was so unfit that after I ordered my own Fitbit online, the bank called to see if my credit card had been stolen! I took that call to mean it was time for me and my family to get moving.

- Got a phone with a camera? Or even an old-fashioned Polaroid camera? Older kids may like the idea of capturing wildlife through their lens. They can learn to capture great photos simply by being quiet, still, and observant while out in nature. They may even choose to enter their photos in one of the many contests, some with prize money, held by nature organizations, from the National Wildlife Federation to The Nature Conservancy.

- Are your kids learning how to spell? Try making the learning process active. Stand on one side of the yard and tell the kids it's a pretend lake or field of lava. Spread out rug squares or other objects to be "rocks" (or use real rocks if they are present) to help your kids cross the lava and have them jump to the next "rock" for every word correctly spelled.

- Need help enticing older kids outside? For teenagers, most everything is better with friends. Encourage them to invite their friends over to play basketball, ride bikes, or go for a local hike. Consider putting up a basketball hoop in the back or front yard (where it is safe from traffic) and watch the magic unfold as neighborhood kids—and your own—are drawn to it.
- If you have a dog, head outdoors with the kids and take them all for a brisk walk. If your kids are old enough, encourage them to hold the leash. And if you don't have a dog, consider getting one—it will keep everyone active and entertained.
- Planning a playdate or a visit with a neighborhood friend? Don't drive—walk to your destination. Once you arrive, spend time outdoors, playing kickball in the grass or making mud pies in the dirt.
- Put on upbeat music and dance with your children every day. Dancing during household chores (indoors and outdoors) makes the duty much more fun. King Julien's lyrics can motivate you while you clean up. Simply replace the lyrics "move it, move it"

with "wash it, wash it" or "dust it, dust it," depending on your chore. Try singing with different accents. The lyrics work perfectly for housekeeping and yard work!

- Head to a nearby park and fly a kite, bat a balloon around, enjoy the playground, go for a short hike, or sled down a hill (with or without snow). Invite your friends. Have an adventure!

- Drive to another neighborhood for a walk. Pretend to be scientists studying a new ecosystem or anthropologists observing an exotic culture.

- Encourage your kids to build an outdoor fort. Supply old blankets, PVC piping, or anything else you have on hand, and let them get creative. Even better, have them use natural materials, such as tree branches and logs.

- Plan a farm "staycation" with your family. Search for locations online and take part in working on a farm. Many places allow younger children to get involved. It's funny how doing chores at someone else's house is considered a vacation, but it works to get everyone moving.

CONQUERING RESISTANCE

As you work on becoming more active and engaging nature, your family may experience a few challenges. Just remember:

Boredom is okay. Life outdoors is not always an adventure. While establishing an agenda will help you stick to it, don't worry about planning every detail for your kids. It's okay if they get bored outside. Boredom lets their minds relax and leads to creativity. When children whine, "I'm bored," tell them that's fine. You might even suggest they count the life-forms they can find; look for things of a specific color, texture, or shape; or just identify the sounds they hear.

Resist the urge to compete. Don't try to keep up with everyone else. Being active outdoors in nature should cost little to no money. You'll find the best items for digging and sorting lying around the house: pots and pans, muffin tins, or spoons. Use your imagination—and encourage your kids to use theirs.

Rethink how your kids are spending their time. If their schedules are filled with activities outside of school—additional classes, sports, other extracurriculars, and chores—consider making changes to allow time for unstructured outdoor play. For example, if your child participates in two indoor after-school activities, consider dropping one. Or find everyday activities your family can enjoy outdoors—even eating outside at mealtime.

Finally, whatever you do outside, expect to get your hands dirty. Ditch the hand sanitizers—just wash with soap and water. We're made to get dirty; enjoy it!

Eat Simply

Balance is not something you find,
it's something you create.

JANA KINGSFORD

FOR ALL THE MODERN TECHNOLOGIES that are supposed to save us time—from washing machines
and dishwashers to cars and computers—life has
only gotten busier. We buy more clothes and
dishes, so we wash them more. We have cars that
allow us to go more places. Computers have man-
aged to ease our tasks while increasing our work-
loads. And many women work full-time jobs and
also primarily take on the double duty chores of
cooking, cleaning, and childcare.

Life has changed drastically since the centenarians were young. Back then, women typically
stayed home, and communities were closer than

most are today. Everyone knew each other, and the adults watched out for one another's kids. Neighbors often baked breads and pies together, and Sunday dinners were social events. One-hundred-year-old Evelyn Reickman remembers her family making meals together. "My two older sisters, Mainy and Vila, were the ones cooking, and they would make tomato soups and cook fried potatoes and all kinds of things. I would help with whatever they needed. We all just pitched in."

Another centenarian, 101-year-old Belen Lopez, was the oldest of nine children and was born near the town of Veracruz, Mexico. "We'd wake up every day at four in the morning to help my mother crush maize to make tortillas by hand. The tortillas were for us to eat, but we'd also sell them to the nearby farmworkers to help us get by. Without electricity or running water, we had many chores to get done . . . everyone helped."

One-hundred-and-one-year-old Amy Sherrard grew up in Burma (now known as Myanmar) as the child of missionaries. One of her favorite items to make and eat was Indian flatbread. "I always made chapati. I especially loved to tear apart that bread and have it with my breakfast.

Not only for breakfast, but any meal. We'd also eat lots of chapati with rice and vegetables." The Indian bread was served at every meal, broken and eaten together by the family (which included her beloved nanny). Ultimately it became a fond food memory for Amy.

We may not be able to return to the communal cooking of the centenarians' past, but we can adopt a few of their practices, such as cooking with whole grains and fresh vegetables; minimizing meat, sugar, and processed foods; and eating together every (or nearly every) night.

In his bestselling books on modern nutrition, UC Berkeley professor Michael Pollan encourages us to stop consuming "pretend food"—food that is ultra-processed and created by industry for consumption. The *real* food, such as fruits and vegetables, is often located on the outskirts of the supermarket and doesn't bear any flashy labels.

Pollan says—and I wholeheartedly agree— that we need to take back control and reduce our dependence on processed food. He suggests following the wisdom of our elders when considering our food consumption: Ask yourself, *Is this an item my grandparent would recommend eating, let alone recognize?*

MODERN TIMES CALL FOR MODERN METHODS

When it comes to meal planning, cooking, and even dining, the rule of thumb is to keep it simple. As children, the centenarians I spoke with ate simple meals primarily made up of vegetables and beans, prepared at home. Meals were high in fiber, largely because of the plentiful seasonal vegetables that were raised in family gardens or grown locally. Meat was a luxury item, so they ate little of it. Often the only choice at breakfast was oatmeal, since it was relatively inexpensive. Very little food was processed or prepared by an outside company.

When asked what she ate as a child, centenarian Lidia Reichel said, "We cooked soup with little meat, and with a lot of vegetables—potatoes, cabbage, corn, and squash, you know—and that was the meal for lunch. And the evening was the leftovers unless we worked hard; something simple . . . maybe fruit, and we baked our own bread."

When we talked with the centenarians about diet, we learned that fiber reigned supreme. One of fiber's major benefits is that it feeds the good bacteria and decreases the bad bacteria in our gut. The gut microbiome, all the thousands of bacteria in our gut, is important to the proper functioning of our body, as well as our overall physical and mental health. Gut bacteria are linked directly to the immune system and can influence many organs in the body, including the brain. Every time we eat something, we are promoting either the good bacteria or the bad.

These bacteria can be altered within twenty-four hours of a diet change. Within seven days, we can completely transform our gut microbiome from one that reflects the modern Western world to one similar to what our ancestors had.

The main way to do that is by eating a wide variety of fruits and vegetables. By eating a range of plant-based foods, we provide healthy bacteria the fuel they need to flourish. It's best to eat something from each of the different groups of fruits (from bright red strawberries to light green avocados), vegetables (from leafy green vegetables to bright purple turnips), legumes, and nuts. Limit meat or use it sparingly to add a little flavor. Incorporate healthier options, like fish, which is high in omega-3 fatty acids and excellent for brain development. To increase vegetable intake, try offering at least two options at dinner or consider making vegetables the main dish rather than a side.

> *Ask yourself,*
> Is this an item
> my grandparent
> would
> recommend
> eating, let alone
> recognize?

Eating produce that is closest to its natural state is best. Each level of processing—from picking the plants, to transporting them, to transforming them into food products, to packaging and storing them—impacts the nutrients they contain. Keep in mind that foods transported long distances are likely not as nutritious as foods grown and consumed locally, because fruits and vegetables begin to lose their nutrient content after harvesting. To eat foods grown as close to your home as possible, purchase them from local farmers markets or grow your own fruits, vegetables, and herbs.

How else can you keep it simple? I suggest the following five steps:

Step 1: Recognize your current practices

Everyone should begin to "keep it simple" by noting their own eating preferences and practices, even vegetarians who think they're eating well.

After all, someone could consume loads of sugary items, cheese pizza, and soda and still technically be considered a vegetarian, though not a healthy one. When Dr. Preet K. Dhillon, senior research scientist at the Public Health Foundation of India, spoke at the Seventh International Congress on Vegetarian Nutrition at Loma Linda University, she explained that research studies of the population in India showed that vegetarians consumed more sugar than nonvegetarians.[1] This phenomenon may occur not just in India but in other countries too.

So whatever your current diet, record your family's eating during a typical week, including all meals, snacks, and beverages. This exercise will give you an idea of your habits and opportunities for change. Another great way to get a bird's-eye view of your dietary practices—and even how they compare to those of the centenarians—is to audit the contents of your refrigerator, freezer, cupboards, and pantry. Think about categories such as fats/oils, meats/poultry/fish/eggs, fruits and vegetables, grains, dairy products, snacks, and beverages.

As you consider what foods to keep in your

house, think like the centenarians: Their food choices not only promote health and resilience, they also prepare them to endure harsh times like pandemics or economic depressions.

So stock your pantry accordingly. Remember, if it's not healthy for the kids, it's not good for you either. Don't store junk food—like soda, chips, and candy—in the pantry, because your family will find and consume it. My daughter Joelle taught me that when she was only four. She was so stealthy that she could have starred on the hit TV show *I (Almost) Got Away with It*, featuring criminals who nearly avoided capture. Early one morning, I wandered into the kitchen to put a dirty plate in the sink. Spying the pantry door ajar, I tried to shut it—but it wouldn't budge. I kept pushing and pushing, but the door stood firm. "What in the world?" I asked.

Looking inside, I spied the top of my daughter's head. She was holding my one-pound Trader Joe's candy bar and quickly shoving pieces into her mouth—as if it were going to be the last bar of chocolate she'd ever get!

But what if your pantry sweep leaves you with few of the convenience foods you often rely on to get dinner on the table at a reasonable time? Do you feel as if you don't have the knowledge or the skills to pull off edible meals for your family? Don't worry—even if you are convinced that the only thing you know how to make is toast, you can make delicious meals yourself with little effort. Or perhaps you do feel highly confident in the kitchen and cook dinner every night. No matter which end of the food spectrum you fall on—from complete beginner to total expert—there is likely room for improvement (whether in making healthier meals, adding more variety, spending less time preparing meals, or teaching other family members cooking skills).

The simpler your meals, the better because preparing dinner shouldn't be a significantly stressful ordeal. In fact, having experience in preparing meals may help you make it through tough times. Anita Johnson-Mackey, age 105, recalled routinely helping her mother in the kitchen alongside her sisters. Though not vegetarians, they ate a lot of salads, greens, and rice and beans. They ate together every night. When she was only ten, however, Anita lost her mom, who passed away during childbirth. "It was fortunate for me that I had already been trained and was able to help take care of things around the house," Anita recalled. "I was prepared."

Step 2: Recognize your feelings

The next step toward a simplified eating pattern is an important and often-overlooked step—to recognize your feelings about this subject. If any of your feelings are negative, recognize them for what they are—just a barrier to overcome.

This may include adjusting your feelings about food preparation. With so many TV cooking shows, it's easy to feel inadequate in the kitchen. After taking a few bites during dinner, my daughter Joelle will sometimes look straight at me and tell me, "You're chopped" (heard on the Food Network cooking show *Chopped After Hours*) if she doesn't think dinner tastes good. Ouch! Talk about deflating my self-confidence!

On the other hand, if you are an expert cook, you might find your kids demanding you serve them a masterpiece every night. If that's the case, reflect on how much time you spend in the kitchen, whether cooking is becoming less joyful and more stressful, and whether or not you demand perfection of yourself. A friend of mine is a single mom who spent so much time trying to make a perfect three- or four-course meal for her daughter every night that eventually nothing she served was good enough—she'd taught her daughter to be as demanding of culinary perfection as she was! Finally, she realized that she no longer loved cooking dinner, and when that happened, she stopped worrying whether it was perfect. She told her daughter that she could eat what she'd prepared or not, but that was what she was serving. Now both mother and daughter are enjoying cooking again, no longer demanding that every nightly meal top the last one.

The goal isn't to become a master chef, or if you are one, to demonstrate all your skills nightly. The goal is to not give up but keep pressing forward—making meals that promote wholeness and supporting others along the way.

I am by no means a master chef, but I gained confidence by using "make it yourself" meals delivered to our home from meal preparation services like Blue Apron and HelloFresh. I choose vegetarian or fish dishes. The produce is typically fresh, and I usually add more vegetables to make the dish go further. The instructions with pictures are easy to follow. Using the "make it yourself" meals is a great way to empower yourself and gain culinary skills. Because of the skills I've gained,

I now feel different about cooking, even venturing out to create meals all on my own.

Another great way to learn how to prepare quick and easy meals is by watching cooking demonstrations on YouTube. Do some searching, and soon you'll find videos by instructors you like who are cooking foods you like in a style that is accessible to you. One chef I follow is Jamie Oliver, who has a cooking show and cookbook on preparing healthy meals with five ingredients or less. See what meals you can prepare with just a few ingredients. The more you experiment, the more creative you'll become.

A busy pediatrician and friend of mine recommended a great source for vegetarian or vegan recipes—the blog and cookbook *Smitten Kitchen* by Deb Perelman. There are a number of other healthy food blogs out there, and with a bit of googling, you're sure to find some that are a good fit for you. With easy-to-follow directions and excellent photos, it's hard to go wrong with these dishes.

Another important feeling to acknowledge and overcome is that you don't have enough time and are already stressed enough as it is. No matter how skilled you are in cooking, you might find yourself dreading the work if you are pressed for time. Keep your meals simple and consider rotating regular meals a couple of nights a week. I make a pot of beans on Sunday and then use them in meals like burritos throughout the start of the week when things are most hectic. I also make extra and freeze portions of dinners for later. I've frozen veggie enchiladas, lentil soup, and even spinach pesto (a great addition to pasta dishes). Some things freeze better than others, so experiment. Pasta and potatoes don't freeze well, but sauces, fish, soups, and leafy vegetables like spinach freeze beautifully.

For some families—such as those with single parents, both parents working outside the home, or kids involved in activities most evenings of the week—finding time to eat together can be tough as well. If you don't routinely have family dinners, start on a weekend night and then gradually add them on one or more weekdays. Older kids may resist having to gather around the table because they want to hang with friends. They may try all kinds of ways to get out of family dinnertime—everything from "I'm not hungry" to "I have to study." Make family dinner an appointment everyone is expected to keep. Let them know that hunger is not a requirement to come to the table, and since the meal may last only twenty minutes, there will be plenty of time to study afterward.

If you are worried you won't have enough time to cook, especially on weeknights, set aside time, just as you would for a medical appointment. Don't book anything within the hour before the meal if possible—this will protect the fringes of time needed to prepare the meal. Encourage others in your house to share the work—either by purchasing groceries, prepping, cooking the meal, or cleaning up. Many hands make light work! You might even take turns on cooking duty with other nearby friends or family members. One night, one family makes the meal—doubling the amount—and either delivers it to the other family or has them over for dinner. Then the families switch.

Not used to eating at home? Start with one meal a week and then build from there. In the end, instead of eating out six days a week and one day at home, try working up to eating six days at home and one day out as a treat. You'll not only spend more time with your family, but you'll also save money!

If you tend to view food preparation as a chore

or busywork, think of it as a gift of time to your family—with all the health benefits from the food itself.

Step 3: Create meal plans

The third step is deciding what meals to make and what foods to select. It's important to simplify foods, options, and tastes and to select food that is as close to the garden and as little processed as possible—choose fruits, berries, vegetables, legumes, whole grains, nuts, and seeds. Foods that will rot are actually some of your best choices because they are in the most natural state and low in preservatives—and you know you have to serve them soon. Even if you have great food skills, take a look at the ingredients you are cooking with. Are your dishes calorie laden—high in meat and carbohydrates but low in fruits and vegetables? Are they high in salt—which ultimately makes them less healthy? Make sure the ingredients you select promote health. Minimize the fat—especially animal fats and trans fats such as vegetable oil or margarine containing partially hydrogenated oil in the ingredient list, as these can elevate cholesterol and contribute to coronary heart disease.

> *Most of your food should come without a label.*

And be sure your meal is high in fiber. Select whole grain breads, rice, legumes, and pasta with higher fiber content. Some great bread choices are seven grain, dark rye, cracked wheat, and pumpernickel. Kids may be more open to eating whole grain breads than whole grain pasta. If your kids don't like the taste, consider adding more vegetables and using less pasta. Don't overlook beans and nuts. The centenarians ate lots of legumes, which include all kinds of beans, peas, and lentils. When selecting rice, brown or wild rice is best. If you enjoy white rice, try mixing brown and white rice together.

Can't read labels and aren't sure of how healthy a product might be? Not to worry! Most of your food should come *without* a label (for example, beans and bananas—no labels there). Although some health enthusiasts tried to teach consumers how to decipher labels so they could select healthier foods, I believe that attempt was slightly misguided. Instead, I recommend embracing the concept of "no label, then it's good for my table." Stick to the food aisles requiring the least amount of label reading—fresh fruits and vegetables. At least start your shopping with the fresh food aisles; that way your cart will have less room for the more processed food items.

One word of caution as you move toward eating fewer processed foods—something I wish someone had told me. While purchasing, storing, and eating more nuts and grains is a great habit to develop, invest in some good, secure containers as well. If you don't, you could end up like I did—battling Indian meal moths that take up residence in your pantry.

The reason these little buggers go bonkers for the stuff is because it's real food. They don't really want the other junk. So make the necessary investments to ward off pantry critters. And keep your nuts in the freezer, where they won't attract bugs and won't go rancid.

Step 4: Dine in

This tip should come as no surprise. Food should not be consumed in a hurry or while multitasking. We have become so accustomed to the feeling of eating on the fly that it seems second nature for most of us. Both my daughter and son try to stuff bagels in their mouths on the way to school each morning. Worried they might get cream cheese on themselves, they usually wipe their grubby hands on the seats in our car. But I must confess, before I adopted the centenarians' dietary habits, I was responsible for aiding and abetting my kids in this. The evidence was everywhere in my car, from straws of various sizes to the array of plastic cutlery and napkins. I also kept giant-size wet wipes, just in case my kids had sticky fingers.

Food should not be eaten while driving, but food should also not be eaten while multitasking at home. How many of us have eaten while performing other tasks? I recently heard of a company that makes it their business to deliver you food while you sit at your computer so you can work while you eat. No longer is there time even to take a break.

It's important to focus on our food when we eat. Otherwise, we tend to consume more calories, and our minds don't get the chance to rest, relax, and connect with friends and family. So the next time you or your family sit down in front of the TV with a plate of food, ask yourself what benefits you are missing. Time with your family? Learning about each other's days?

The delicious taste of the food you prepared? Chances are, you're missing a lot if dinnertime means TV time!

Step 5: Drink water

Simply choose water—it's the best choice all around. It doesn't come in dynamic packaging or with fancy-colored dyes that are cause for parental concern; instead, it is virtually free or inexpensive. Invest in a durable water bottle so you can carry water with you wherever you go. When I asked my husband's great-aunt, centenarian Mulan Tsai, what she likes to drink, she answered with a smile: "Water."

"What about tea?" I replied. "Don't you like to drink tea sometimes?"

She shook her head and said, "No, just plain water." Throughout our interview, in fact, she sipped on a glass of water as if it were the elixir of life—which it is.

Curiously, throughout history, none of the government food guides really promote water consumption. The latest USDA guide, My Plate, includes sections for protein, grains, fruits, vegetables, and dairy. Where's the water?[2] After all, the adult body is made up of 60 percent water (a newborn is made of even more—78 percent), and water is so critical to life that we would die within a few days without it. It also has no calories, making it the perfect drink for kids and adults.[3] Why then isn't water included? It should be, particularly because we aren't getting enough.

In America, approximately 75 percent of adults and 54 percent of children are chronically dehydrated, hindering our bodies from functioning properly and setting us up for a number of chronic diseases.[4] The latest edition of the American Dietary Guidelines (2020–2025), released by the USDA, indicates not only what we should eat but also what we should drink to stay healthy. It recommends drinking "beverages that are calorie free—especially water."[5] This statement is a step in the right direction in encouraging us to consume water.

We are bombarded with all kinds of drink options in every color of the rainbow and for every activity, whether we need a boost in the morning or play a specific sport. All the popular drinks for kids contain lots of sugar (usually in the form of high-fructose corn syrup), lots of calories, and potentially harmful dyes.

For the centenarians, who had limited incomes

and limited access to well-stocked grocery stores, these unhealthy drink choices just weren't available—and thankfully so.

In living more like the centenarians, I've cleaned up my own pantry and fridge, getting rid of the sodas and juice boxes I once routinely kept on hand. My children don't even ask for them anymore. A few times I've observed both my daughter and son looking in the pantry, then looking in the fridge, like they were on a search for the Holy Grail. They inevitably gave up and decided to quench their thirst with ice water.

READY, SET, GO!

Are you ready to discover the healing power of foods and family mealtimes? Would you like some tips on how to eat delicious, healthy foods that fit within your budget and time limitations? Do you want to promote resilience and enhance balance in your own family? Are you ready to draw on the wisdom of these ancient elders, the centenarians, and raise healthy, happy children? If so, let's get going!

- If you don't have much experience with cooking, order vegetarian meals to make at home (like from HelloFresh or other meal preparation services) and use this strategy to gain skills. We get two meals a week from one of these services. My daughter likes helping out with the meals, and I enjoy the time we spend together.

- Explore lunchtime finger foods. Send a sack lunch to school with your child at least once or twice a week rather than always relying on the school's lunch choices. Include a variety of healthy food items (apples, tangerines, carrots and hummus, sliced cucumbers or celery, peanut butter and jelly sandwich [if no peanut allergies] or veggie burrito) in fun sandwich bags. Bento boxes contain many small compartments for a wide variety of food. Include a thermos with water.

- Want a quick idea to ward off hunger pangs? Have snacks that can satisfy your need for crispy or sugary sweet delights readily available in the pantry and fridge. Nuts, dried fruit, and vegetables can give you a variety of textures and tastes and are far healthier than chips, crackers, or chocolate bars. After grocery shopping, chop veggies and put them into baggies so they are ready to use throughout the week.

- Looking for a simple way to encourage young kids to eat veggies? Light candles at each meal (not just dinner) to make the environment fun. Then let those who eat the most vegetables blow out the candles.
- Make an oatmeal bar with ingredients from your pantry. Include toppings like dried cranberries and blueberries and a range of nuts. Want sweeter oatmeal? Provide a little honey, cinnamon, or fresh fruit.
- Go meatless at least once a week. If your taste buds find that difficult, try a meatless meat product available at the grocery store. Substitute these for meat occasionally, but remember that fake meat is still processed food. You can also substitute beans or legumes for meat in chili and soups two to three times per week.
- Get outdoors at breakfast, lunch, dinner, or snack times! Build on your active movement principles and take your food fare outside. Have a picnic in your own backyard or at a local park. Pack simple, healthy snacks for your picnic. Choose foods with brain-building omega-3 fatty acids such as chia seeds (fun and yummy to dip fruit into),

edamame, salmon, and trail mix with wal-
nuts. Your child's brain—and behavior—will
benefit. Don't worry about planning all day;
even spontaneous picnics (ready in fifteen
minutes) can be fun!

CONQUERING RESISTANCE

Picky eaters. You might encounter some resistance
from your kids as you try to change their diet plans
and habits, especially those who don't want to try
anything new. One approach that has helped in
my house is a rule requiring our kids to take two
"no, thank you" bites of food. They can't just out-
right reject something without taking two bites. In
fact, when the centenarians were children, it would
have been unheard of to reject the food their parents gave them. They not only worked hard and
were hungry, but they knew that whatever was set
before them was their only option. Like the centenarians, the more today's children are exposed to
new fruits and vegetables, the more their palates
will adapt and accept them. So don't give up. If
you feel as if you make multiple meals in a single
evening because your family members have different tastes, simplify your approach. Make just

one dinner, which can include many vegetable and fruit side dishes. That will increase the likelihood that everyone finds something they like.

Snack attacks. Your children may come to you right before dinnertime, complaining they are hungry. If you want them to have something, offer the fruits and nuts you've set out on the counter, or provide a vegetable tray with hummus for dipping. If they don't want to eat the veggies, they likely aren't too hungry. Reduce their dependence on snacks to encourage them to be hungrier at mealtimes.

Packed schedules. After the turbulent start to this decade, watch out for that pesky feeling that you need to make up for lost time. Feeling this way may increase the likelihood of overscheduling activities like sports or music lessons. Resist the urge to add extra activities that could crowd out family mealtimes.

Rest and Reset

*It's all about finding
the calm in the chaos.*

DONNA KARAN

MOST OF THE CENTENARIANS my fellow researchers and I interviewed were from farming families
whose waking and sleeping habits were tied to
their work. More than one hundred years ago, it
was easier to rise and go to bed according to day-
light hours, and people slept an average of nine
hours each night.[1] One centenarian I interviewed,
101-year-old Dr. Ellsworth Wareham, recalled his
childhood mornings: "I'd routinely rise between
four and five-thirty in the morning every day to go
out to find and then milk the cows before eating
breakfast and then heading off on the two-mile
walk to school." Later in life, as a heart surgeon,

he remained disciplined, working well into his nineties.

In contrast to Dr. Wareham's experience, our kids are more likely to sit for most of the day, whether that's at their desks in school, in front of their laptops, or in front of the TV. As a result, their bodies aren't expending the energy that the centenarians did at their age, which made it easy for them to fall asleep.

In addition, the light, noise, and air pollution of our modern world increase the likelihood of their sleep being interrupted. The internet and other technology make it harder and harder for our kids to shut their minds off before bed. The light from computer screens and smartphones also disrupts the production of melatonin, the hormone that regulates our sleep/wake cycles.

We now sleep an average of less than seven hours a night,[2] and many people either struggle to fall asleep or drift off the instant their heads hit the pillow. (It should take five minutes or so for the brain to make the transition from wakefulness to sleep.) This generation requires more help and planning to protect and encourage beneficial, restorative sleep.

Just look at all the ads on TV for products

guaranteed to improve sleep—ranging from mattresses to medications—and all the books and blogs with ideas to help you fall asleep more quickly and sleep better. Consumers spent about $41 billion dollars on all these products in 2015, and this number is only expected to increase.[3]

Not only do Americans sleep less than their elders did, many Americans no longer take much vacation time, if any, losing out on an opportunity for restoration. In 2018, 55 percent of Americans reported unused vacation time and a whopping 768 million unused vacation days.[4] Employees in other countries, including Japan, China, and South Africa, report taking even less vacation time.

From my perspective as an epidemiologist who studies social connections and their impact on health, one way I measure our society's values is through the advertising that targets our needs and desires. Based on that, I have to conclude that although we recognize our "unfortunate" need for

> *Sleep deprivation has become the new normal, but it comes with dire consequences we have yet to fully understand.*

sleep, we place greater value on staying busy. Sleep deprivation has become the new normal, but it comes with dire consequences we have yet to fully understand. If we continue on this path, what lies ahead for our children's mental, physical, and spiritual well-being? It's time to change our view of rest by looking at the centenarians' practices and how we might implement them within our own families.

MODERN TIMES CALL FOR MODERN METHODS

Though as children the centenarians lived in a world in which it was much easier to find time for rest, we can still adopt some of their practices to promote resilience within our own families. Let's take a closer look at their three rules for resting and resetting:

Step 1: Establish a routine

Though we often think of sleep deprivation as mainly an adult problem, research shows a link between chronic sleep deprivation and detrimental health conditions in children. Decreased sleep is linked to increased body weight, insulin resistance, and elevated stress levels. Scientists have uncovered

a link between sleep loss and the risk of developing diabetes and obesity. A 2002 study of 8,274
Japanese children ages six and seven showed that
fewer hours of sleep increased the risk of childhood obesity.[5] Researchers have hypothesized that
sleep deprivation may permanently disrupt the
hypothalamus—the region of the brain responsible for energy expenditure and appetite regula-
tion. New research also shows that children who
lose on average just an hour per night in sleep may
be at greater risk of developing diabetes.[6]

In addition to adverse physical health conditions in kids, sleep deprivation can also hinder
the mental and social aspects of everyday life.
According to a recent research study led by a
Harvard pediatrician, children in preschool and
elementary school who don't get enough sleep
are more likely to have problems with attention, emotional control, and peer relationships at
around age seven.[7] Because sleep deprivation hin-
ders the ability to pay attention and concentrate,
it should come as no surprise that sleep is also tied
to achievement in school. As children get older,
staying up later to cram for exams doesn't necessarily produce the desired outcome. Too many late
nights can lead to excessive sleepiness and hinder

academic performance—not to mention perfor-mance in extracurriculars like sports and music.

One-hundred-and-one-year-old Salma Mohr told me, "We were always in bed by 9:00 p.m. Mother started shooing us off to bed after 7:00 p.m. since this was around the time our kero-sene lamp would go out. There was no special fuss-ing about getting to bed. Each day was consistent, going to bed and rising at the same time."

In fact, the majority of centenarians I spoke to were from farming families, so their sleeping and waking habits were routine, even on weekends. Even non-farming families like Salma's rose early every day of the week.

Anita Johnson-Mackey, age 105, said, "We were taught to go to bed at a certain time. And no staying in bed in the morning. If we said, 'But I'm tired,' I could hear Mama saying, 'Well, maybe you'll remember to go to bed earlier. But you're getting up now, young lady.' And that was that."

A recent article in *Scientific Reports* explains the importance of maintaining a routine sleeping pat-tern. Inconsistent schedules like getting up earlier on weekdays while sleeping in on weekends cor-related with smaller gray-matter volume in several regions of the brain in early adolescents.[8] Later bedtimes on weekends were also associated with poorer grades.

As you begin to establish a routine, start by assessing your family's evening and bedtime habits. Do you have rules you abide by to ensure everyone gets to bed at a decent time? For younger children, a good bedtime is usually between 7:00 p.m. and 8:00 p.m. Keep in mind that children tend to fall asleep faster when they get to bed before 9:00 p.m. Once you set your bedtime limits, stick closely to them. Canadian researchers found that the children with parents who followed strict bedtime rules had better sleep.[9] Make sure older children are off their computers and cell phones at least an hour before bedtime. The Screen Time app, available for both Apple and Android users, will enable you to disable your internet at a certain time. Several other apps, such as Net Nanny, BreakFree, unGlue, and Spyzie parental control, also allow you to limit your kids' screen time and block their access to unsuitable content.

During the day, do your best to be sure you and your family get outdoors and are more active. The natural lighting outside helps our bodies fall asleep more quickly in the evening. The sooner and the more often you get outdoors throughout the day, the better chance natural lighting has to improve your sleep.

Don't schedule too many activities close to bedtime. Plan ahead to allow plenty of time for your kids to complete big school projects so none of you have to cram to finish them the night before they're due.

Step 2: Take a moment (relaxation)

Be sure that relaxation—pausing to find peace and downtime for the mind, body, and spirit—happens throughout the day. It is crucial to take breaks and allow our minds and bodies a moment to decompress. We are bombarded by emails, phone calls, text messages, television, and commercials. We rarely have a moment to let our brains get bored or wander.

I asked 105-year-old Anita Johnson-Mackey how she took breaks when she was young. Her eyes lit up and she replied, "Reading!"

With so many adventures to choose from in books, reading gave her comfort and escape from daily life. As an African American, she faced unique challenges as a child. "We lived not in the Black neighborhood but in a white community, which was hard for my family," she told me. "So early in life I always had a library book to take a break. I liked to go to the library to relax and read too. That was the one place we could always go, and Father felt it was a respite from the world."

Allowing our minds to take breaks comes with so many benefits, especially for stirring creativity. All types of innovative people, from scientists to famous authors, have experienced "aha" moments during periods of relaxation. Albert Einstein and the surrealist painter Salvador Dalí were known for taking walks in nature during the day to help relax their minds and come up with new ideas. In his memoir *On Writing*, Stephen King said his book *Misery* came to him while he was taking a nap on a plane.[10] Johannes Brahms wrote symphonies, and it is said that naps at the piano helped him write his most famous lullaby—ironically a song notable for putting many children to sleep. Even companies like Nike and Google are catching on to the idea of rest for the mind by encouraging workers to take naps during the workday to stir creativity.

Planning kids' days so they have time for adequate rest and unstructured playtime will allow their minds to rest, wander, and daydream—increasing their creativity, whether they're interested in science, math, or the arts. Such downtime will decrease their stress levels and make it easier for them to fall asleep in the evening. In addition to enhancing creativity and promoting independence, restful periods during the day are linked to a variety of health benefits. In a study of elementary school children, midday napping (not too late in the evening) was associated with "higher happiness, grit, and self-control"; reduced behavior problems; higher verbal IQs; and better academic achievement.[11]

To promote relaxation and rest, learn to value the white space on your calendar. Leave it open for spontaneous activities or simply for relaxing with family and friends. Such time often makes for the best memories.

One important practice of the centenarians is always taking one day of the week to relax. They often refer to this as taking a Sabbath moment. This day of rest is not intended for lazy behavior or goofing off; rather, it's a needed break for the body, mind, and soul.

Since adapting our lifestyle in the past few years, our family shuts off the electronics and attends church rather than spending the day parked in front of the TV and computer. After the service, we often head out for some mountain biking or hiking in the south hills. The change has been so remarkable that now, if ever we miss spending this quiet time together on the Sabbath, we really feel the weight of increased stress when we start a new workweek.

Rest and relaxation enable us to better deal with the day-to-day stressors of life. When your body is allowed time to rest, it can use that time and energy for restoring itself. Research has shown us that the immune system works best when the body has adequately rested.

> *Rest and relaxation enable us to better deal with the day-to-day stressors of life.*

Step 3: Create restful space (restoration)

Organize your home to support a peaceful, relaxing state of mind. Your home can become a sanctuary away from the hustle and bustle of the working world. Decluttering will increase the feeling of peace and restfulness as soon as you enter the front door. If you are pressed for time, consider cleaning the area you see first when walking into your home.

When we visited my husband's great-aunt, Mulan Tsai, one of the first things I noticed was how inviting her house was. The front entryway was filled with jade plants and potted orchids, which provided a sense of serenity and beauty. The sun shone through expansive windows, and the rooms were simply decorated with beautiful Asian furnishings. Her home was neat, tidy, and peacefully quiet, with no television blaring. It was similar to many of the other centenarians' dwellings I visited, which had entryways and living rooms furnished and organized to foster a relaxed state of mind.

If you find it hard to keep your home neat and clean, consider hiring a housekeeper to help out once a week—and if that's too big an expense, just once a month can make a huge difference. Better yet, do as the centenarians did with their kids—get them to pitch in and help clean up the house as a part of their regular chores!

READY, SET, GO!

To foster rest, relaxation, and restoration, you can try some of these tips.

During the day:

- Avoid caffeinated beverages late in the day. Drinking caffeine may make it more difficult to fall asleep. And remember, many sodas and sports drinks contain caffeine—one reason children can be hyperactive.
- Limit simple sugars like candies, cookies, and sodas. Such foods will give you an immediate sugar high and then cause you to crash. Prevent these dives by eating less of these foods—or cutting them out altogether.
- Take breaks outdoors. Routine exposure to natural light during the day will help you fall asleep faster at night.

Before bedtime:

- Remove phones from all bedrooms or turn them off.
- Avoid artificial screen light right before bedtime. If you want to unwind in bed, read a good book, but no more Netflix in bed.
- Put on relaxing music in the evening to set the stage for transitioning from the hectic day into bedtime.

- Work as a team. Involve your partner in helping children get ready for bed. This underscores that sleep is a family priority. One of you can read a book to your kids or make up a bedtime story. One of my friends told me that her ex-husband would call their five-year-old daughter just before her bedtime. He would then tell her a special story, one that grew more elaborate every night. The daughter couldn't wait for bedtime to hear the next chapter in this continuing saga—and it always helped put her to sleep (while keeping her close to her father, who lived in another state).
- Establish and stick to routines. Kids thrive on them. For young children who start the day between 6:30 and 7:30 a.m., a bedtime between 7:00 and 8:00 p.m. is entirely normal.

In the bedroom:

- Turn on white noise. If you or your family members fall asleep more easily to the sound of the ocean, crickets chirping, or a steady rainfall, consider getting a white noise machine.

- Use blankets and coverings appropriate for the weather. Change them when the seasons change. According to the Sleep Foundation, the best room temperature for a good night's sleep is around sixty-five degrees Fahrenheit.[12]
- Keep water near the bed. Children often wake up in the middle of the night, wanting something to drink. Consider giving them a water bottle they can keep nearby. This is equally important for adults, since many people are dehydrated by the morning, which may put them at greater risk for a heart attack and many other medical issues. If you wake up during the night, reach for your water bottle and drink up.
- Make sure pets don't wake up your family at night. High-energy dogs and nocturnal pocket pets like hamsters or hedgehogs may be restless and noisy. If you have any of these furry party animals, keep them out of the bedrooms. During the day, give your high-energy pooches plenty of exercise, such as a longer walk or jog, to tire them out.
- Keep things simple and consistent. As children, the centenarians didn't rely on

products to help them sleep. Instead, they spent plenty of time outdoors being physically active, and they followed routine, with strict early bed- and waking times.

To relax and refresh:

- Take a noonday break and head outdoors to sit or take a quick walk. While you're there, blow some bubbles, which helps the body relax. When you need a break at work or school, take a moment to look out the nearest window. Try to observe a grassy area, a tree, or other vegetation. Now imagine yourself outdoors experiencing that "secret garden" with all your senses. Imagine the sun on your face, or the blades of grass under your feet. Count to ten and then journey back from your secret garden to the present. I used this trick in eighth grade math class whenever I was overwhelmed and needed a quick break.
- Encourage your kids to grab a puzzle or a coloring book and sit quietly near a large window or—even better—head outdoors.
- Spread a blanket on the ground in your yard, lie on your back, and check out the clouds.

Make a game with your kids of pointing out all the different shapes, objects, and animals the clouds are making.

- If your children lie down for a nap and ask you to lie next to them, take the time to do so. Don't worry about all the dishes in the sink or the office work to attend to. Breaks are good for them and for you!

- Routinely combine a great book with a night-time stuffed friend to help younger children transition into bedtime. One of my favorite books to read at bedtime is *Good Night, Gorilla*, accompanied by a stuffed monkey. When I'm done reading, I tuck the monkey in first, followed by my daughter.

CONQUERING RESISTANCE

Be prepared to overcome the barriers you may encounter as you implement and maintain your relaxation and resting goals.

Holiday hustle. Holidays—particularly Christmas and Thanksgiving—can be a mad rush for the whole family. Make sure to build in downtime, especially for younger kids.

"Just one more." Kids are great negotiators. Be

prepared for them to try stalling or derailing rest or relaxation habits. Be consistent and firm, particularly with your bedtime routines.

Pandemic times. Older children may be more reluctant to go to bed when routine schedules are thrown out the window—as was the case during the COVID-19 pandemic. My teenager began staying up later and later, trying to connect with his friends through any electronic device available. Be alert for this behavior and stick to your bedtime routines—it's best to be fully rested to help ward off infection.

Cultivate Life-Giving Relationships

Ohana means family. Family means nobody gets left behind.

Lilo & Stitch

IT IS WELL-KNOWN THAT OUR FRIENDSHIPS can help protect and sustain us. The centenarians I interviewed had strong social networks and nurturing, lasting relationships, many of which had started in early childhood.

During my interview with one-hundred-year-old Reynaldo Sanchez, he picked up a picture of his special childhood friend and told me, "We've been friends since we were four years old. He is my friend from a long time, and I love him as [a] brother."

All of the centenarians reported strong social ties, especially with their family members but also with neighbors and church members. As children, they spent time together helping with farmwork, as well as community and church work. After their daily work was done, they played and socialized by reading together, telling stories, or playing cards or board games, and their deep friendships provided emotional and physical support to help them navigate early adversity.

Even the animal kingdom understands this concept. Take, for example, the penguins living in the harsh conditions of the South Pole, where temperatures reach sixty degrees below zero and the wind speed is up to one hundred miles per hour. If you and I were placed in that environment, we would quickly freeze to death. The penguins, on the other hand, have a strategy that helps them thrive—they huddle together for warmth. The temperature at the center of their circle is about seventy degrees.[1] Like penguins, we can't make it on our own; we need to come together to thrive.

African elephants also demonstrate how to work together. The females don't raise their calves alone. The older elephants adjust the pace of the herd so the young can keep up. When a calf is injured or missing, several members of the herd assist in the search and rescue. Equally impressive is that elephants that haven't seen each other for years will recognize their long-lost friend, even decades later, and act as if they'd never been apart. These rich relationships help them weather any storm.

Researchers have theorized that family stories are an important part of shaping the emerging identity and well-being of the children.[2] To test their theory, they created the "Do You Know?" scale for kids to assess their family knowledge, including such questions as: *Where did your parents meet? Do you know where your grandparents grew up? Do you know what high school your parents attended?* My kids laughed when they learned my favorite childhood toy was a doll that I named after the family car: "Babot Collada Chevrolet." Scientists have found that the more children know about their family history, the better connected they are, the higher their self-esteem, and the more control they feel they have.

MODERN TIMES CALL FOR MODERN METHODS

Let's take a closer look at three essential steps to cultivating life-giving relationships and discover how to do them with our own kids.

Step 1: Make it a priority

One of your most important responsibilities to your children is teaching them to value meaningful relationships, as well as modeling the skills and time they require. The earlier in life these skills are learned, the better. Prioritizing nurturing relationships means routinely connecting with others, being present in the moment, and actively listening. It means reaching out, not only in the good times but also when immense hardships hit and connection is needed most. Finally, we must be able to physically see or hear the other person. Being together in person is best, but if that is impossible (as it was during the pandemic or when living far apart), use electronics (like Zoom or FaceTime) that promote hearing, seeing, or both. Though it's quick and easy to text and send emails, those messages often cause more confusion and put you at greater risk of miscommunication, especially when relationships are already strained. With our frenetic pace of life today, it's easy to put other pursuits before spending time with our family and friends, but positive relationships are worth the time.

When I asked centenarian Anita Johnson-Mackey if she sat with her family at dinnertime, she replied without hesitation, "Always. Always. No running into the kitchen, uh-uh. We sat down at the dinner table all together. And my father wanted to know what had happened during the day."

We can't make it on our own; we need to come together to thrive.

When Anita's family sat down for dinner, they reflected on their experiences that day and discussed whether they'd faced any challenges that needed to be handled differently. This practice had likely been passed down through her father's family line—a powerful legacy.

You have to be present to invest in others, so make the people in your life a priority. A friend of mine sets a timer in her house to go off as a reminder to hug her daughter, who has special needs. The benefits of those hugs are immediate, as they calm her daughter and help maintain a sense of peace in her home.

We accomplish more and greater things by working together. Think about the way geese fly in a V formation. Scientists have found that the birds position themselves this way and beat their wings in time with their neighbors to catch the preceding bird's updraft and save energy—using up to 40 percent less energy and reaching their destination sooner.

Belen Lopez, age 101, learned the value of working with others as a little girl. She grew up in a home that lacked running water, so every other day, she and her siblings walked one kilometer to reach the nearby river. Rather than looking at their walk as a dreaded chore, she always looked forward to the outing. The river provided so much for the family—not only was it a place to wash clothes, but it also gave them the opportunity to hang out with friends, cousins, and neighbors. On the shore, some people boiled water and cleaned clothes, while others took their makeshift fishing poles and worked at catching fish for a shared lunch. After collecting water for drinking, cooking, and bathing, they made the trek home. This communal way of life, of everyone helping each other, gave Belen a sense of security.

Step 2: Show up with love

Encourage your family (and yourself) to respond to every experience with kindness and tolerance.

This means not only showing up with love for others, but offering love to yourself, too.

When centenarian Salma Mohr was a little girl, she loved going to school. Her older siblings had dropped out of school after seventh grade and gone to work to help provide for the family. They cleaned houses, and her older sister was known as one of the best housekeepers in their community. She got eight dollars a week to clean houses, a top salary for that work then.

"When I got up to the seventh grade," Salma said, "it was my turn to give up going to school and find a job. I just grieved. I must have shown it to my sisters. *Oh, if I could just go finish the eighth grade. Oh, if I could just finish the eighth grade.* And my two older sisters put their heads together and they said, 'We've got to manage and let Salma finish the eighth grade.'

"Well, then I got to go to high school. But in my mind, I knew that this wasn't going to last very long, and I'd have to drop out before I could finish it. So I arranged with my teachers, and they helped me finish in three years; I was sixteen. And then the moping started all over again."

Fortunately, Salma's sisters came through again with love and support.

"And it was so funny because at that point, I had to earn the money for books and pay for college. And of course, I didn't have that. So the two older sisters and the two older brothers put their money together to buy my schoolbooks and helped pay my way."

Salma's siblings loved her so much that they worked hard to make her dream of education come true. Salma eventually became a teacher.

I think of that kind of love whenever I pass a prominent statue on my university's campus that depicts the biblical story of the Good Samaritan. Jesus told a parable about how a Jewish man was attacked, beaten, robbed, and left for dead while traveling from Jerusalem to Jericho. The first two men who passed by him were religious leaders. Neither stopped to help. Then along came a Samaritan. Because Samaritans and Jews were sworn enemies back then, hearing about the Samaritan's kindness would have shocked Jesus' listeners. The Samaritan scooped up the injured fellow, placed him on his donkey, took him to a nearby inn, and paid for his care.[3] Like the centenarians' experiences, this parable encourages each of us to lay down our judgment—whether against others or ourselves—and embrace one another with boundless compassion. Showing up with love begins by taking the initiative to connect with others, just as the Samaritan did.

Not everyone will look the same or believe the same. But we all are human and want to be heard and loved. Recently, my daughter Joelle confided that she ate alone at lunch for a while when she changed schools several years ago. Eventually, she made new friends, but it took many months. Knowing how sad it made her, she vowed to encourage other newbies and to be a smiling face they could connect with at lunch. At first, it was hard for me to hear that she'd eaten alone all those months. Our inclination as parents is to jump in and solve things, especially when it comes to mealtimes—we are truly the knights of the lunch table. But if Joelle hadn't gone through this difficult time, she might not have discovered this passion for helping others—or purposefully shown up with love. Over the years her group of newbies has grown, and she has developed wonderful friendships. Now, whenever a new girl arrives at school, the administrator is quick to introduce her to Joelle and her friends.

Another critically important aspect of showing up with love is tolerance—the willingness to see others' opinions and expressions without reacting adversely, even if you don't agree with them. As parents, we need to step back and ask ourselves, *Am I modeling tolerance and encouraging it in my children? Or am I quick to jump in with a furrowed brow and tell someone why their view is wrong and then try to convince them that my view is right?*

Centenarian Anita Johnson-Mackey's advice to parents is to "be slow to respond to something that may look offensive." It's better to respond by saying, "Why, I never thought of it that way," and then listen with respect for the other person's point of view.

Step 3: Use high-level connections

High-level connections are those interactions in which you are "with" each other. By seeing or hearing additional verbal cues and responding with your own, you can be truly present.

The centenarians didn't have our technology. When they related to one another, it was usually face-to-face. The time we spend with friends and family, especially our children, has a tremendous impact on their present and future, but it takes concentrated investment. When a child asks you to sit on the floor and play, do you spare a moment to engage with them? When your teenager excitedly tells you about an accomplishment at school, do you stop what you're doing to listen and affirm them? When you do, you are making investments in their lives, creating stronger bonds with them, and giving them a sense of security. The earlier in their childhood you start connecting with them in this way, the better.

During the COVID-19 outbreak, many communities were ordered to "shelter in place"—a public health mandate to reduce the spread of the deadly virus. In such times it is especially important to connect and encourage one another because many people feel isolated and alone. People found creative ways to reduce exposure but remain connected. Children used washable paints to write hopeful messages on their windows, or they hung signs encouraging those who passed by. Other people drove by loved ones' homes with birthday greetings. I heard of one couple expecting a baby who drove past friends' homes to do a gender reveal announcement, honking the horn

Not everyone will look the same or believe the same. But we all are human and want to be heard and loved.

of their car, which was decked out with a pink sign and balloons. Other people used Zoom to hold virtual dates. They played a board game, ate a meal, or baked together remotely. Some people dropped off notes on neighbors' doorsteps with their phone number and encouraging words. We learned it's possible to connect and practice social distancing; it just requires a little creativity.

We can create inviting spaces in our homes to promote connectivity too. My great-grandparents were Danish, and I appreciate their emphasis on *hygge* (pronounced "hue-guh"), or creating an atmosphere of coziness or comfort that promotes connectivity and friendship. Other countries, from China to the Netherlands, have their own words to describe this feeling. Each boils down to the desire to create inviting spaces that encourage people to spend time together enjoying the moment.

Cozying up your own home can help set the stage for spending more time relaxing with family and friends. You don't need to remake your entire home; start simply by adapting one room. I made my living room more welcoming by moving in a rocking chair from another room, positioning the chairs and couch to encourage conversation, and adding a large basket to hide toys (baskets can hide a lot). Board and card games are tucked away but easily accessible when company arrives. I've also added soft, thick blankets and oversized pillows to encourage cuddling and relaxing.

Consider other areas of your home that could easily be made cozier. For instance, lighting candles at meals will help set a warm atmosphere. Setting out a swing and chairs on your patio will make it an inviting place for outdoor conversation. By making these small additions, you are encouraging slower, more relaxing activities with family and friends.

READY, SET, GO!

The busier your life, the more you need routines to ensure that connecting with others, especially your family, remains a priority. Here are a few ideas to get you started!

- Plan a backyard movie night with friends and family (to connect with each other and nature), complete with a few yard games. Invite acquaintances who are new to the neighborhood or parents you've met in passing at your child's school.

- Have a child celebrating a birthday? Consider throwing a centenarian-style birthday party. Host a smaller and more intimate party with family and a friend or two. Take a simpler DIY approach, perhaps holding it outdoors with a nature scavenger hunt.

- Keep compact card games stashed in your purse or glove box for a quick bonding game with kids or friends. You'll be prepared whenever you need to kill some time, remedy boredom, or distract the kids and get them to settle down!

- Send a friendship challenge card in your child's lunchbox and encourage them to build positive friendships. One day a card might encourage them to say hello to a new person at recess, while the next day a card might encourage them to say something kind to a friend. If they can't read yet, simply draw pictures. Remember to ask them about their experiences after school.

- Dinnertainment, anyone? Keep a box with conversation-starting questions near your dinner table. My five-year-old niece likes this activity so much that when she sits down at my table, the first thing she asks is if we can start a conversation.

- Have your older kids carry a "friend in need" ziplock bag and be on the lookout for others needing help. Within the bag, keep small, useful items for helping in a pinch: Band-Aids, wet wipes, coins, a small amount of cash, tissues, rubber bands, and breath mints.
- Create a simple art project with your kids, perhaps using items from nature like leaves, flowers, or feathers, and present it to someone feeling down to show them your love.
- While driving your kids to and from school, why not strike up a conversation? Stash the cell phones, turn off the radio, and ask open-ended questions like "What was one of the best things that happened to you today?"
- Teach your children the value of connecting through handwritten letters. Or have them color pictures and mail them to their grandparents, relatives, or friends as a welcome and unexpected surprise. Get some stamps and send cards for birthdays.
- If you have older children, take part in an activity that interests them. If they like to

play a strategy game, play it with them. If they enjoy biking, ride along with them. Conversation will flow more easily, and you may find an activity you can enjoy together for many years.

- Have a standing appointment for a potluck dinner or luncheon gathering with family and friends. Scheduling a recurring meal one day a week or a month is a great way to ensure you get together regularly. Don't worry so much about the menu; focus more on getting together.

- When visiting others, bring them flowers, coffee, or a bag of oranges to brighten their day. Be sure to ask about their children and family. Encourage your older children to ask questions and listen for answers too. When the visit is over, help tidy up, especially if you have children who have made a mess.

CONQUERING RESISTANCE

As you work on connecting with friends and extended family, you may experience a few challenges yourself. Here are some ideas to help you overcome such resistance:

Introvert challenges. Are you an introvert at heart? Do you find it difficult to branch out and meet new people? If so, take simple steps to increase and strengthen your social connections. Start small and seek out groups that interest you, or reach out in places where you are already connected (like your child's school or a house of worship). Plan a playdate to get to know the parents of a child with whom your son or daughter has hit it off. When you meet new people, ask about their interests or family and then sit back and let them talk. Remember to be yourself and enjoy the moment of connecting.

Work challenges. Be wary of taking on additional responsibilities at work. Be careful of accepting new assignments that will require you to take home paperwork or stay later at the office. Before saying yes, consider how this decision might impact the time you have to spend on your children's health and happiness.

Build a Foundation of Faith

Live simply, love generously, care deeply, speak kindly, leave the rest to God.

ATTRIBUTED TO RONALD REAGAN

THE CENTENARIANS I interviewed all reported early exposure to and affiliations with Christian, faith-based communities, which provided them—and often their families—with support, stability, and strength in times of great adversity. They even supplied socialization and entertainment.

The centenarians mentioned several daily and weekly faith practices. They routinely thanked God for their food before each meal and prayed again at bedtime. Their weekly practice included attending a house of worship, reading the Bible, and volunteering in church ministries and their communities. Their faith seeds were planted early in life, though as young children they didn't fully understand what it meant to have faith in God. As they grew older, however, they began to develop a deeper faith connection.

Dr. Mildred Stilson, a vibrant centenarian, described her life as being faith-informed. "We are here to serve," she told me. Born to missionary parents, Mildred grew up in India, where her dad was a pastor and later became a physician. Watching her parents help others and take part in India's cultural activities helped Mildred understand how service is a way to live out our faith.

"I felt called to follow in the footsteps of Jesus and his ministry work, helping to heal people," Mildred explained. She was so inspired by her faith and her parents' service that she went on to medical school, where she was one of only seven women in her class. She became a pathologist, a physician who uses tissue and blood samples to diagnose a wide range of diseases. Feeling a higher calling, she became a missionary, just like her parents before her, and served in Africa. Mildred's early upbringing and experiences with her faith influenced all aspects of her life, a tradition that she passed on to her own children.

Research has shown that having a faith connection can reduce stress and anxiety and even boost happiness. A systematic review published in the *Journal of Religion and Health* looked at decades of published articles and confirmed the association between faith and happiness.[1] Studies have found that families with a regular connection to a faith community have greater satisfaction with their lives, better problem-solving skills for health-related problems, and more family involvement than those who attend less regularly.[2] Additionally, praying frequently outside of formal religious services was linked with a reduction in the risk of depression and anxiety.[3] A faith connection has also been linked to decreased feelings of hopelessness and suicidal thoughts and behaviors.[4]

Not only does joining a faith community boost happiness and reduce the risk of depression in children, it's great for parents, too! A study of more than 74,000 women who attended a religious service more than once per week found that they had significantly less cardiovascular- or cancer-related mortality compared with those who never attended.[5] A study of the same cohort discovered that women who attended Catholic mass more regularly were less likely to commit suicide.[6]

A 2012 study of 17,705 adolescents discovered that regular faith connection with a house of worship was associated with a decreased likelihood of substance use behaviors (like alcohol, drug, and tobacco use) as well as decreases in the likelihood of fighting, theft, and delinquency.[7]

In addition to these scientific studies, when I surveyed other moms and dads, they told me they regularly participated in church because they liked their children to connect with other kids outside of school. (The busier mom side of me was quick to realize that when the children connected in this setting, it was so much more relaxing—for both Mom and Dad and for the kids—with no scoreboards to monitor or loud, obnoxious cheering needed. What a relief!) The parents also appreciated meeting other parents with shared beliefs, helping their children learn better behavior and increase their confidence through interactions with positive peers, seeing their children gain valuable life skills through volunteering, and being able to sing and enjoy the musical experience together. One of the most common responses was that they appreciated the support their faith community provided—through faith, they found friendships that supported them in their successes, losses, and life challenges. The house of worship can provide enormous strength.

MODERN TIMES CALL FOR MODERN METHODS

Let's take a closer look at three steps for building a strong foundation of faith for your children.

Step 1: Connect with the Higher Power

Some great ways to find guidance on your spiritual journey and grow closer to God are by developing and strengthening your relationship with a house of worship, reading spiritual texts (like the Bible) to gain new insight and knowledge, and praying out of a sense of need, repentance, thanksgiving, or even just to dialogue with God.

In the world the centenarians knew as children, all communities were tied together through faith. However, things are different today. As technology rapidly advanced and people became more mobile, regular worship often took a back seat to prosperity and other pursuits, and involvement in faith communities declined just when society needed those connections most. Unfortunately, the number of Americans who claim no faith affiliation is rising. The global researcher World Values Survey determined that between 2007 and 2019, forty-three of forty-nine countries became less religious.[8] According to *National Geographic*, the newest major religion is in fact no religion at all.[9]

Nearly one-quarter of Americans questioned at the start of the COVID-19 pandemic said their faith had grown as a result[10]—though the strength of the impact and how long it will last have yet to be determined. With the increase in natural disasters, possible terrorist attacks, future global disease outbreaks, potential severe economic depressions, and the hectic pace of modern society, we need a connection with a faith community more than ever. Scientists have uncovered tremendous benefits from connecting with a faith community, especially for promoting lifelong resilience.[11] A number of studies have shown that youth and their families who regularly attend a house of worship have better coping skills and are more satisfied with their lives and more involved with their families—all of which helps them to endure challenging times.[12]

The centenarians know far too well the pain caused by significant hardships and loss, both as children and adults. Centenarian Salma Mohr described in great detail the loss she experienced as a young child. She prided herself on being the caretaker for the youngest sibling in her family— baby Maxine. One day, Salma's littlest sister became extremely sick. "She was very, very ill and had a terrible temperature," Salma told me. "But evening came, and her temperature rose even more. Mother made my other brothers and sisters go to bed. But I had refused. I couldn't go and leave little Maxine because I think I had the real genuine mother's heart for that child. I stayed till I got sleepy; I don't know what time. But way over in the middle of the night, I could hear my father crying with a horrible voice—he was heartbroken."

Salma crept out of her own bed and tiptoed down the hallway. "I listened for one minute and then I ran off to my bedroom because I knew what had happened. I started crying too. Little Maxine had died in the night." Salma's family, her faith, and her connection to a house of worship helped her cope with her immense loss.

When she was twelve, Jane Pihl (now age 102) got up one day in her Lincoln, Nebraska, neighborhood to learn that every bank in the United States had closed—a horrific event that would long be remembered. That morning, the community's

Kids who regularly attend a house of worship have better coping skills and are more satisfied with their lives and more involved with their families.

Union College Chapel became a gathering place for people in absolute shock. "I mean everybody came up to Union College Chapel. I'll never forget it," Jane explained, the memory of the comfort she found in her community of faith still palpable ninety years later. The people in her community didn't have much left, but they clung to their church, faith, and prayers to help ease their burden and fears.

The start of the Great Depression was so devastating that "people were jumping out of windows," Jane recalled. People had lived through the Roaring Twenties, but now in 1929, they were panic-stricken. Many lost everything. Jane's dad was a landscape architect, and one of his customers went out into a field and ended her own life. Finances became tight for Jane's family, too, since no one hired a landscaper when they had no money. Their faith helped them to weather the storm. Perhaps you might be fearful today of the possibility of a new Great Depression following the COVID-19 pandemic, and a faith connection—just as for Jane and her family— could help your family weather the storm.

Whether you are already part of a faith community or aren't currently interested in connecting with one, I encourage you to read on. You may be surprised by the hidden benefits.

Step 2: Connect with a house of worship

Centenarian Salma Mohr looked forward to attending her local church. She would head there every week, whether or not anyone went with her. "I was just five or six and lived close to the church and would go to the church every Sunday," she said.

For centenarian Anita Johnson-Mackey, connecting with her church meant crossing the railroad tracks and walking a long way. "I crossed the tracks and went to the Black neighborhood to the wonderful, well-kept African Methodist Episcopal church." It was this church and its community that gave her family a feeling of connection and protection.

The key is to find a place that feels right for you and your family. One size does not necessarily fit all. Even if, for some reason, you are not ready to connect with a house of worship, I encourage you not to let that stop you from seeking a closer connection to God.

Despite the many benefits faith communities offer in a world filled with rapid technological advances and the resulting stress, far fewer families today connect with faith communities than when the centenarians were children. There are numerous possible reasons for the decline. Many families spend their weekends involved in the children's extracurricular activities, particularly sports teams, many of which now practice or compete on Saturday and Sunday mornings. Other families, especially those with young children, may not notice a direct benefit from attending church. Given all their other responsibilities, going to a house of worship every week becomes just another thing to do. Some may feel their kids aren't that interested in attending, so why bother.

At the start of the pandemic in early 2020, many families that were attending adapted to worshiping online when houses of worship closed. In fact, many people relied on these streaming services to find hope and remain connected to their faith communities. Unfortunately, some of the health-related benefits of attending services are lost when the community moves totally online. If your family has never or rarely attended church, considering doing so. Following the pandemic, you will likely be in the company of many others who are reconnecting or who are going to church for the first time.

If we don't become active with a faith community when our children are young, we are not caring for their spiritual health or planting and nurturing the spiritual seeds that will serve them as they grow. The amazing thing about seeds is that you don't notice the dramatic changes that are taking place beneath the surface once they're planted. But those hidden changes are necessary for the plant to produce fruit.

Step 3: Extend your connection

You can draw closer to God not only through involvement in a faith community but also through prayer and reading spiritual texts. Many of the parents I interviewed agreed that one key benefit of being part of a faith community is the many people who come together to pray with them during challenging times. Prayer draws you closer to God and gives you guidance and strength.

The scientific community has done many studies on the health-related benefits of prayer.[13] They've uncovered its effectiveness at reducing feelings of stress and anxiety.[14] Taking a moment to pray in the morning will help you set the tone for the day. Do you or your family have difficulty going to bed because your minds are so busy that you can't sleep? Are you a multitasking worrier—concerned about your health, your kids, your work, or the many challenges impacting the world? Then bring your worries to God before going to bed each night and throughout the day to give your mind and soul needed rest. You might keep a prayer journal to record your requests and the way God answered. Reading back over it can renew your hope whenever you're faced with new difficulties.

Teach your children to pray and encourage them to turn to God, especially when faced with challenges that bring them to tears. Encourage them to pray before taking tests, before important events, and throughout the day. Once, my kids and I even prayed for a new dog. As we stood in the middle of the San Bernardino animal shelter, surrounded by a chorus of barks and whimpers, we said a quick prayer, asking God to help us choose a dog that would be a great fit for our family. Jayden added, "Please give us a dog that can do tricks."

My son then noticed a small, gray, dirty, poodle-looking dog at the back of a cage with three other pooches. Once the kennel assistant removed the disheveled dog from his cage, I gently lifted the mangy hair hanging over his face to make sure he had two eyes. He looked a hot mess and smelled much worse—a dingy old mop for sure. My son said to the man, "We'll take him!" And that was that.

Fast-forward a few years, and we realized we had a beautiful, fluffy, white bichon poodle mix we'd named Mr. Beans. He happened to be the

When we shift our thought patterns by praying rather than fretting, we build new neural pathways in our brains that help us worry less and cope better in moments of stress or anxiety.

smartest and friendliest dog we'd ever met. Best of all, he quickly learned to do tricks! So teach your children to be specific in their prayer requests. Also remind your children to thank God and express gratitude to him when they notice his blessing or experience his love and grace.

Whenever you clean up behind your kids or tuck them into bed, take a moment to say a quick prayer over them or ask God to bless them. These small prayers will shift your way of thinking— from focusing on the chores in front of you or your worries for your children to a mindset of gratitude and dependence on God. When my husband does the laundry, he says a prayer and asks for bless- ings as he gently places each child's clothes into the washer. (And I say a prayer that he doesn't mix the reds with the whites!)

A quick prayer doesn't require extra time, just a different thought. And when we shift our thought patterns by praying rather than fretting, we build new neural pathways in our brains that help us worry less and cope better in moments of stress or anxiety. Let's face it, we could all use less stress and worry. Why not give it a try?

The answers to our prayers aren't always what we want or expect; sometimes they are hard to accept and even shake us to the core. But God can use the bad experiences, as tragic and heartbreaking as they are, to help shape us and get us to the point where we need to be in order to fulfill his purpose for our lives. God doesn't promise that he will keep us from the fire, but he does promise to walk through it with us. As my centenarian friends discovered, faith and prayer can give us resilience, help us weather storms, and lead to outcomes we may never even have imagined.

READY, SET, GO!

Building a strong faith foundation can make a world of difference in your kids' overall well-being—and yours as well! Here are a few ideas to get you started:

- When you sit down for dinner, invite your family to pause for a moment and take turns saying a prayer, thanking God for your meal. You might also encourage everyone to mention one good thing that happened to them that day. A vegan Mexican restaurant in West Hollywood, Gracias Madre, takes being thankful to a whole new level. Before even ordering their meal, patrons must say: "I am thankful for . . . [whatever item they want to order]." The waiter then replies, "Yes, you are thankful for . . . [restates the items ordered]."

- Pray daily when rising in the morning or going to bed at night. Keep a prayer journal and jot down your requests and their answers.

- Practice a meditative prayer walk when heading outdoors for exercise. Pick a place a few blocks away and then walk or jog there. Begin praying on the way. When you reach the destination and turn around, meditate on your prayer and listen for God's response.

- Curl up with your children to read a spiritual text together, one that is age appropriate for them. Even better, take a blanket and the book outdoors to read together.

- Spend a day outdoors with family and friends in nature. Bring along some snacks to eat as you share a simple devotional.

CONQUERING RESISTANCE

As you work on strengthening your kids' faith foundation, you may experience a few challenges. Consider these ideas to overcome the resistance:

Not a "spiritual" person. You don't have to feel spiritual to attend a house of worship. Every person is embodied with a spirit, and it is important to find ways to promote resilience for that part of you. If you don't feel ready to visit a house of worship, consider gathering outdoors with friends or family to read Scripture while connecting with nature.

Fear of the unknown. Going to a church for the first time reminds me of heading off for the first day at a new school and worrying that you'll be sitting alone at lunch. A great strategy for overcoming fear is to partner up and not go alone. Get your spouse on board and go together as a united front. If you are a single parent, invite your own parents, another nearby relative, or a friend to come along. Keep in mind that if it doesn't feel like a good fit, you don't have to go back—but do keep looking for a house of worship to connect with.

Too tired. Feeling exhausted after a long week of events that kept you on the go? Keep in mind that attending a house of worship will reenergize you and give you an emotional and spiritual boost.

Too many other activities. If you feel your family doesn't have time, reevaluate how loaded your schedule is. You and your family need to nourish and develop your spiritual—along with your physical and mental—well-being.

Kids aren't interested. To appeal to young children, try finding a church with an outdoor playground or indoor play space. To get older children interested, try suggesting they invite a friend along or go to a church where their friends already attend. With the allure of a playground or a meetup with friends, your kids may end up begging you to go to church each week.

Develop a
Positive Mindset

*It always seems impossible
until it is done.*

NELSON MANDELA

ONE FEATURE OF THE CENTENARIANS that stands out is their tremendous focus and grit. Believing their actions would result in positive outcomes, they set goals and persevered to reach them, despite countless obstacles. Whenever I asked centenarians about challenges in their lives, they'd inevitably say something like, "I didn't have any challenges or hardships." But their life stories are filled with all kinds of difficulties, both as children and adults. Yet they chose to focus on the good things rather than the hardships. They were grateful for simple experiences, blessings, and opportunities, seeing the positive in each situation.

You only have so much room in your brain, and when you fill up the space with negative thoughts, you have little room for positive ones. You and your children need to catch yourselves when you begin to focus on negative thoughts so you can make room for better ones. Pay attention to the frequency of your negative thoughts and when most of them occur—is it in the morning, afternoon, or evening?

The key is to break the cycle. When you catch yourself thinking negatively, shift the dialogue in your brain. Think of something positive or how you might view the challenge constructively. As 105-year-old Anita Johnson-Mackey said, "Don't get angry at hardships; try to look at them as learning opportunities."

While working as a professor and overseeing online schooling for my kids (the schools had mandated closures due to the pandemic), I received a telephone call. The local county health department needed more epidemiologists and asked me to come and help in the battle against COVID-19. Helping the county would truly test my ability to stay positive.

At times the situation became overwhelming with cases rising—not just globally and nationally, but in my own community. Two thousand positive cases were identified in my county over just one weekend. The hospitals and ICUs were filling, and the death toll was rising. As I felt myself moving into a rut of despair, I knew I needed to get my mind together to keep up the good fight, so I took the advice of my centenarian friends and regularly headed outdoors with my kids. As we took a brief walk

Each one of us is more powerful than we give ourselves credit for, and the impact you and I can have on our own lives and those of others is unimaginable.

around the block, I'd say a quick prayer for health and healing for my family, for our community, and for our world. My mind and spirit immediately felt better, and my children were happier too.

The centenarians didn't allow difficult circumstances to limit their mindsets or influence their behaviors. They chose not to settle. They focused on their goals, determined to achieve them. They persevered despite all the setbacks and doubting people who told them their ambitions were impossible, and your kids can too!

MODERN TIMES CALL FOR MODERN METHODS

Let's take a closer look at the three steps to developing a positive mindset—focus, positivity, and gratitude—so you can start using them with your own family.

Step 1: Focus your steps

Each one of us is more powerful than we give ourselves credit for, and the impact you and I can have on our own lives and those of others is unimaginable. But don't focus on the unimaginable—think of all that you and your children might do. Find ways to tap into your mind and use it for good—doing so will encourage your children to do the same. Don't let major challenges, limited resources, or outbreaks stop you and your family from reaching your goals.

Life brings a series of dreams and goals; whenever you reach one, set an even bigger one. Dr. Ellsworth Wareham, now age 101, had a goal as a teenager to go to college—and he did! Then he decided to go to medical school. Then he chose to train in heart surgery when few training programs were available. Later he traveled to perform open-heart surgeries in underdeveloped countries around the world. At each stage, he reached his objective and set another. When individuals set ambitious goals, not only will their lives change, but they can literally save lives, as Ellsworth's career trajectory demonstrates.

Ellsworth was a teenager during the Great Depression and grew up in a community in which nobody went to college. But he saw going to college as his only option—it wasn't a matter of whether he could go or not; it was only a matter of what he had to do to get there.

The same was true for mountaineer Hulda Hoehn Crooks. With no formal training, she decided to teach herself to climb mountains. She first climbed Mt. Whitney at the age of sixty-five—and scaled it another twenty-two times—making her final climb at the age of ninety-two. Just the year before, at ninety-one, she climbed Mt. Fuji, the highest peak in Japan. Now she holds world records. It wasn't a matter of whether she could or should hike these mountains; it was only a matter of what she had to do to reach the top.

Step 2: Cultivate positivity

The second step to achieving a positive mindset is engaging in positive thoughts, speech, and action.

A positive mindset starts with positive thinking, which just means approaching difficulties more constructively, optimistically, and productively. You think the best is going to happen, not the worst. When things don't go according to plan, you see the setback as a temporary situation. In contrast, negative thinkers—those who are more pessimistic—are more likely to blame themselves or others when bad things happen. They tend to expect negative outcomes and assume the fallout will last for quite some time. Negative thinking may seem normal and harmless, but it actually works against people's ability to succeed. If you persistently think negatively about yourself and your abilities, you can actually increase the likelihood of a negative outcome.

Does positive thinking really make a difference? Absolutely! Even if you or your family members don't naturally look on the bright side, there are ways to cultivate positive thinking.

A great way to encourage positive thinking is to start by promoting positive self-talk. Even professional athletes know the importance of practicing a positive mindset, and they participate in training sessions on cultivating positive self-talk techniques. Scientific studies support the belief that how you think about your performance, before and during the event, will influence your outcome.

A recent study of 117 athletes—across a wide variety of individual sports (like gymnastics, swimming, and wrestling) and team sports (like volleyball and ice hockey)—was conducted to assess the impact of positive self-talk on athletic performance. Athletes were assigned either to the control group, with no special intervention, or to groups who received one-week or eight-week self-talk intervention in addition to the usual training. Researchers discovered that those who practiced positive self-talk performed better than those who did not, and that the more self-talk they engaged in, the better they did.[1] Imagine that—thinking and speaking your way to victory!

The study concluded that positive self-talk is associated with greater self-confidence, less anxiety, greater self-optimization, improved self-efficacy (a person's belief that they can accomplish what they put their minds to), and better performance. Moreover, by participating in the study, the athletes learned to increase their attention on the thoughts running through their minds, promote positive self-talk dialogue, and reduce interfering thoughts. They learned to recognize their emotions as they engaged in self-talk and to focus during training and competition. When children learn to practice positive self-talk early, they are more likely to have a growth mindset—the belief that their intellectual abilities are adaptable and that they can rise to the challenge.

Another great way to promote a positive mindset is to consciously let go of regret, anger, worry, and bitterness—*just release it*. Let go of the toxic feelings so the healing will come. If you made a mistake, someone hurt you, or life doesn't seem fair or isn't turning out the way you planned, don't dwell on it.

In Disney's *The Lion King*, the lion cub, warthog, and meerkat sing "Hakuna Matata," Swahili for "there are no troubles." No matter what happens, promote a positive mindset by shifting from a focus on your troubles to a focus on your opportunities. Don't fret. Centenarian Amy Sherrard was the child of missionary parents and often faced the unexpected. She said, "You have to have a geographic spirit. You plan to the nth degree, and as soon as you press the start button you go with the flow."

Turning to God in prayer can help you release negative feelings and shift your mental focus.

Prayer can help ease your burden and lead to a sense of hope and support—and the very act of praying can help you articulate your problem and the solution you are seeking.

Allow yourself and your family time and space for positive learning experiences—*just learn it*. Take up a hobby, learn to play a new musical instrument, or enjoy the arts, which can all help relieve stress and build skills. The more you develop your abilities, the more confidence you will gain and the more you will realize that you can achieve what you set out to do. Positive learning experiences will shift your focus from hardships to a state of peace and relaxation.

Recognize your child's strengths and give them opportunities to develop them. Most of the centenarians had hobbies from early on, which brought them comfort and joy. Anita Johnson-Mackey (105) and Dr. Mildred Stilson (100) took to reading, and Jane Pihl (102) played piano.

Finding your child's interests starts with conversation and observation to discover what they like. What activity have they told you they'd like to try? What do they naturally take to? Do they have artistic talents? Musical talents? Can they take things apart and put them back together? Are they physically gifted in a sport or dance? Once you have a good sense of their natural talents, look for local classes or training opportunities. The key is not to push them toward activities you want them to excel at but rather allow children to guide themselves toward their own interests.

Step 3: Embrace gratefulness

Going hand in hand with positive self-talk and thinking is an attitude of gratitude. To be grateful is to notice your blessings, no matter how big or small, and to be thankful for them. Centenarian Salma Mohr didn't have much as a child, but early on she learned not to complain. Instead she expressed gratitude for even the smallest things. She recalls not having a doll of her own, but rather than feel deprived, she treasured the thrill of just touching the hair and dress of a neighbor friend's doll. Then one day, she found her own treasure.

"On our way to school we had to go through an alley. And each day we would pass by everybody's garbage along our walk. And one day, of all things, I found in the neighbor's garbage can the most gorgeous pieces of broken glass. And I could tell by some of the larger pieces that it must have been a glass plate or bowl. And it was clear and blue."

Salma carefully scooped up the pieces and took them home, where she kept them in a special box. She would often take out her blue pieces of glass and shine them up with a cloth. "Oh, that was my first treasure I ever owned. On sunny days I would carefully take them outdoors and let the sun shine through them and put new spots everywhere. That was my toy." What one person had thought was a useless bowl, broken and without a purpose, became a young girl's prized possession. Despite how little her family had, Salma developed a grateful perspective.

Centenarian Anita Johnson-Mackey also remembers learning as a child not to complain. As an African American living in a white community in the early 1900s, she could have held on to a number of grievances. But she realized that though she didn't always have control over her situation, she did have control over her attitude.

"I learned early in life, if something came up, don't be complaining at all," Anita told me. "And ask yourself, *Did I have anything to do with this? What can I do about it now?*" This mindset and approach to hardships served her well. Later, while working for Veterans Affairs as a medical social worker, Anita encouraged her clients to change their inner dialogue from complaining and defeatism to one focused on gratitude, action, and positive change.

When I'm tempted to let all the difficulties I'm facing get me down (especially when I was caring for my family while helping to battle COVID-19 in our community), I often think about Nick Vujicic. Nick is an international motivational speaker from Australia who is famous for his positive outlook on life and upbeat attitude despite his enormous challenges.[2] He is one of only seven individuals worldwide living with tetra-amelia syndrome, which is characterized by a lack of arms and legs. When he was born in 1982, his parents—Boris and Dushka—were

Even when disappointments happen and life doesn't go exactly as planned, we can be encouraged when we remember that what may seem unfortunate initially may turn out to be a blessing in disguise.

heartbroken. After overcoming their emotional distress, Nick's parents were determined to give him the most normal childhood they could. From the beginning his parents instilled the importance of always being thankful for what he had, no matter the situation. Nick grew and learned to do things most other children were doing, but in a slightly different way. He was a rough-and-tumble young boy, and one of his favorite activities was riding a skateboard flat on his stomach, towed behind the bicycle of his brother or a friend. Though his parents worried he would injure himself, he typically replied, "It's not like I'm going to break an arm or a leg!"[3]

Though bullied as a child, Nick was determined to succeed in everything he put his mind to. Still, he spent his childhood and teen years feeling lonely and depressed. But as a young adult, Nick found faith through prayer, and his attitude turned from self-pity to self-actualization. He began speaking at schools spreading a message of hope, especially for students who were bullied or facing tremendous difficulties. In 2005, at the age of twenty-three, Nick founded Life Without Limbs, an evangelistic organization. A few years later he developed the school curriculum Attitude is Altitude to spark passion and hope around the world with a core message that our attitude determines our ability to succeed. Nick has since married, had children, and lives a life of true abundance. He uses his personal experience to inspire others to action. He proves that no matter your circumstances, you can make positive changes and be an overcomer.

Even when disappointments happen and life doesn't go exactly as planned, we can be encouraged when we remember that what may seem unfortunate initially may turn out to be a blessing in disguise. A traffic jam might have kept you from getting to your destination on time, but that backup might have prevented you from a collision with a distracted or reckless driver. A job opportunity might have fallen through, but it could have been an unexpectedly bad fit, or a better opportunity could come along soon. Even a difficult "sheltering in place" mandate during the COVID-19 outbreak led to some positive benefits—within just a few months, some wildlife began making a comeback, and the air pollution was almost extinguished in many areas of the country.[4]

When we stop focusing on our misfortunes, weaknesses, and faults and start acknowledging and being thankful for all the good things in our lives (including what we are doing right), our mindsets will shift from dashed expectations and disappointment to appreciation and positive thinking.

A great way to start acknowledging your blessings is by keeping a gratitude journal. Studies have found that writing down our feelings of gratitude results in immediate health benefits and leads to a more positive mindset. In two university studies, two hundred undergraduates were split into three different groups, each with a different writing task.[5] One group was told to record their blessings; the second to record their hassles; and the third to record their experiences in general. Participants in the gratitude group felt better about their lives overall and even began looking forward to the upcoming week. Not only did they feel more positive emotions, they were more likely to help someone in need of emotional support or with a problem. A Polish researcher discovered that counting and recording our blessings each day can reduce feelings of stress.[6]

If journaling doesn't appeal to you, think of other strategies to document or notice the blessings your family experiences (like writing them on a chalkboard, jotting them down on sticky notes and placing them on the fridge, or reflecting on them over dinner or at the end of each day).

Recalling the positive events and blessing in our lives was especially useful during anxiety-ridden times like the COVID-19 outbreak. The news and social media focused on counting the numbers and discussing the tragedy. While it is good to be in the know, it's better to keep our central focus on the positives rather than concentrate on the uncontrollable variables around us.

READY, SET, GO!

- Develop a family motto with your spouse and kids; encourage them to start each day on the right foot by stating this motto.
- Practice following up every negative thought with a happy one. Notice throughout the day when you have a negative thought. Then either state your motto to yourself or respond with a positive comment. You can also take a step outdoors to help change the negative dialogue loop in your mind.
- Take a moment and visualize yourself accomplishing a great feat. Imagine what

the accomplishment feels like. What friends, family members, or other individuals surround you? What are they saying?

- Keep a gratitude journal. Jot down daily all the blessings in your life that you are thankful for. Make it a family affair and encourage your kids to add their thoughts.

- Make gratitude into a fun game. During dinnertime, see who can come up with the longest list of things they are grateful for. Parents can even share things they were grateful for as children. Have simple prizes handy for a few categories, like the longest list or the craziest or most interesting blessing.

CONQUERING RESISTANCE

As you and your family work on strengthening your positive mindset, consider the following ideas if you face any of the challenges below:

Too many Eeyores. Eeyore, the donkey character in the *Winnie-the-Pooh* books by A. A. Milne, inevitably finds the bad in everything. He hangs his head, he moans and complains, and no matter how good things are, he finds a reason to be depressed. Let's face it, it's downright tough to be around people who are Eeyores. But that doesn't mean you need to abandon them. They need your positive attitude and words to encourage them to shift their outlook. Watch your own thoughts and emotions when you are around these people, but continue to take up the challenge of trying to bring them back to a positive place.

Consecutive setbacks. If you feel as if you have gotten stuck in a rut and nothing you are doing is working, take a time-out. Give your mind a break and recharge your batteries. Once you do, you can reapproach the problem through prayer or by developing a specific motto to repeat and focus your mind as you tackle the challenge again.

Worrying about what other people might think or say. Remember that when others begin to observe all the benefits of practicing a positive mindset, they may want to join you.

Help Others

*The best way to find yourself is to lose
yourself in the service of others.*

MAHATMA GANDHI

FROM AS YOUNG AS AGE THREE, the centenarians
often had chores around the house and on the
farm. Farming was a physically tough way of life
that required everyone to pitch in, from planting
seeds and harvesting crops to tending livestock.
Children's work was real and valued. Young children often helped prepare the food and care for
younger siblings. More than half the centenarians reported that as children they were responsible for cooking, cleaning, and sewing clothing
for church members, students, teachers, and community members who temporarily stayed in their
homes.

Their families were also engaged in church activities and ministries, which they viewed as opportunities to help others, especially the poor— even if they themselves didn't have much. Family members were always ready to jump in and act whenever someone called for help, even at the last minute. The drive and willingness to help others was a seed planted early in the centenarians' child- hoods, and it matured and bloomed throughout their lives.

In earlier times and even in developing coun- tries today, toddlers learn to help out. In rural areas of Africa and Asia, it isn't at all unusual to see tod- dlers bringing sticks to the fire to help their moth- ers or grandmothers cook, hauling small pails of water from the river, or tying dolls on their backs to prepare them for carrying younger siblings when they're older.

While taking on such responsibilities is not as common in the West, it's wise to remember that even very young children can help. We often assume they aren't capable, but by giving them small tasks, we are planting the seed that tells them they can. In fact, they usually want to help—we just discourage them because more often than not their help leads to more work for us! But do give them a chance—the extra effort now will pay off as they grow older. Toddlers who practice mixing cake batter may be able to make pancakes for the family when they are six or seven. Preschoolers who learn to put their toys away before bed are more likely to develop a habit of picking up after themselves.

When my son was four, he could deadhead my rosebushes and trim back other plants with blunt-tip scissors. He even cut one of my loveliest bushes into the shape of a cartoon character—unfortunately,

By taking part in chores, children begin to focus less on themselves and more on others.

I had no prior knowledge of his detailed plan. By the time he went to kindergarten, he had some of the best scissor skills in his class. The point is, by helping me, he helped himself!

MODERN TIMES CALL FOR MODERN METHODS

Let's take a closer look at how you can get your twenty-first-century kids excited about helping others.

Step 1: Connect with their what

The first step in getting your kids to actively look for ways to help others is identifying their talents and how they can share them with those in need. Have you ever thought about what special gifts your kids might have? A special gift can be just about anything that is unique or creative. Even time and a willingness to help are gifts that can be shared with others.

I like the story of one boy who shared his time and passion to promote positive change. In the seventh grade, Craig Kielburger read about Iqbal Masih, a child slave who'd worked in a carpet factory in Pakistan. After learning that bonded labor was declared illegal by the Supreme Court of Pakistan, ten-year-old Iqbal escaped from the factory where he'd been forced to work and led a campaign against childhood slavery. Tragically, however, he was killed two years later.

Craig shared the story with his class, and many were moved to act. Along with eleven of his friends, Craig started a charity called Free the Children. Without money or financial backing, they got right down to business by bringing awareness to the public and government officials about indentured children around the globe.

"Kids are looking to get involved. They're searching for it," Craig said.[1] He felt that something as important as making the world a better place, especially for children, would take everyone pitching in, not just grown-ups, and he was determined to do his part.

During our interview, centenarian Dr. Mildred Stilson told me about her early life as a child living at an altitude of seven thousand feet in a remote little village nestled in the Himalayan mountains. When her parents moved there as missionaries in 1916, they were the only Caucasian residents. They had arrived at a chaotic time. The First World War was already raging in India, and the man who was supposed to meet them to tell them what to do and where to go had died unexpectedly when the ship he was on was torpedoed in the Mediterranean Sea.

Without his guidance, her parents first learned the language and then worked many years not fully knowing what they were doing in India. Mildred's dad had always been interested in science and providing basic medical care, beginning with bandaging his own pets' wounds. Once he was able to talk in their own language to the village schoolboys with whom he worked, they started coming to him with medical needs. He was the only one around who had any knowledge of what to do when someone had been hurt badly. Once more villagers realized that her dad could help take care of sick people, many sought him out. He once estimated that he devoted only half his time in India to his work as an ordained minister; he spent the other half at the dispensary tending to the sick.

"When my sister and I got to be about six, seven years old," Mildred told me, "he started inviting us to come help him." The girls rolled up their sleeves and made cotton balls and bandages to assist their dad in his care for the sick. This instilled in Mildred a desire to help others.

"I think the biggest thing it did to me as a child was make me realize how very, very fortunate I was. And it made me realize that what I really want to do is something that will help reach people wherever they are on the earth, whether it's South America, India, Indonesia, wherever," she said. "They have a life that is so hard compared to the joy and privilege that I have, that I couldn't possibly think of just living the rest of my life doing only for myself."

Mildred went on to complete medical school and then returned to the mission field as a physician. Imagine if everyone—adults and children—shared their gifts, talents, time, and compassion with the world. Doing for others can positively change life for yourself, your family, your community, and even the world.

Step 2: Connect with their where

Once you've identified what your kids can do to help others, the next step is to look for opportunities for them to get involved—and then do it! Your family can take action at three levels: your household, your local community, and the global community.

One of the first places children can learn about leaning in and lending a helping hand is in and around the home. By taking part in chores, children begin to focus less on themselves and more on others. However, in today's society, most housework is done by one or both parents (usually the mom) or even a professional housekeeper. Research conducted by Dr. Richard Rende, a developmental psychologist, found that though 82 percent of US adults had to do family household chores when they were young, only 28 percent have their own children help out with chores.[2] Other countries like Canada, China, and the United Kingdom are also experiencing a similar shift in decreasing help from children with chores.[3] Gone are the days when children were referred to as "Mommy's little helper." Many parents today don't see the need for or the benefit of having children take part in chores. Often, they don't feel they have the time or the energy to supervise their children or to make sure they do their chores.

Kids' whining and complaining only increases the reluctance of many parents to expect them to help keep the household running:

> "Do I really need to do it?"
> "But she doesn't have to do it, so why do I?"
> "I *can't!*"

As a result, moms and dads may decide it's just easier to take care of the housework themselves rather than tackle household chore negotiation. By excusing children from helping, we may finish the cleaning more quickly; however, our children will miss out on the hidden benefits that come from contributing to the household. In his book *Raising Can-Do Kids*, Richard Rende says the tendency to assign kids fewer chores is troubling, given its importance to social and behavioral development.[4] The extra effort by parents is well worth it—even if it's a daily challenge.

After studying various indigenous communities in Mexico and Central America, psychology researchers from the University of California, Santa Cruz, reported on a division of housework in these rural communities that was similar to what the centenarians experienced in their childhoods.[5] They observed children three or four years of age helping out alongside adults and older siblings. They coined the term "learning by observing and pitching in" to describe the young children who took the initiative to help after watching others around them. These kids were already collaborating with their families and communities in a range of complex activities, such as cooking, running errands, or tending to younger children. Their parents' goal was for the children to become responsible contributors to their families.

Working alongside family members was an important feature of the centenarians' upbringing as well. Tasks were focused on "family care" rather than "self-care." For example, when it was time to fold the laundry, one or more children were tasked with folding all the clothes, not just their own. Our kids are capable of more than we think.

One way to make household chores more fun for younger kids is to play music and tie it to the completion of the task. For example, clean one room in the time it takes to play a song, or vacuum the house in just five songs. Mary Poppins—the nanny in Disney's musical film—understood the value of reframing a child's approach to household chores. "In every job that must be done, there is an element of fun. You find the fun and—snap!—the job's a game." As they tidy their nursery, Mary sings along with the children, "Just a spoonful of sugar helps the medicine go down in a most delightful way."[6] Why not put on some Mary Poppins and clean along with her delightful, energizing songs?

Older children who haven't been assigned many chores in the past may need time to get into the habit, but continue encouraging them and give them more complex and age-appropriate tasks. They may be able to help with mowing the lawn, cooking a meal, sewing worn clothing, washing the dishes, and even buying the groceries (supervised, of course).

To encourage older kids, let them know they can earn rewards such as that beloved computer time or a special activity. While working together, you might tell them about the chores you did at their age—and how they differ from today. You might also take a trip to a local heritage center or historical museum to get a taste of what chores were like back in the nineteenth century.

Not only does completing chores help build strong family connections, it also provides physical activity. The centenarians stayed active and strong in part through household chores. Moving, bending, stretching, and lifting are all part of keeping a home and yard in order—and are just what you need to keep your body limber.

According to the Center for Parenting Education, another important benefit to chores is that they teach life skills, like doing laundry or making dinner.[7] Children who don't learn these simple tasks grow up to be dependent on others to do them. Everyone—males and females—should know how to cook their own meals, clean their own homes, and wash their own laundry. Of course, teaching these tasks can be time-consuming—for both you and your children. I was once concerned that if my kids helped with chores, it would take away from the time they needed for homework and other activities. But once I made clear that helping out at home was expected, they got on board (despite the moans and groans). I quickly discovered that many chores can be done in twenty minutes or less. More importantly, children who learn to complete tasks at an early age are much more likely to be focused and productive later in life.

Before assigning chores to family members, get their input. Also, ask yourself if anyone is ready to learn a particular life skill (like cooking, buying groceries, doing the laundry, or mowing the lawn). Don't expect them to do chores that are beyond their cognitive or developmental abilities, but do give them a chance to be challenged. If they screw up—and they will—don't scold them; encourage them. Point out what they did right, praise them, and let them know they are going to get better the more they do it. And avoid gender stereotyping— girls need to learn to mow the lawn and repair things, and boys need to learn how to fix a meal and do dishes.

If you or your spouse currently do most of the work in your house and yard, you may need a mindset change just as much as your kids do. Let go of the standard of perfection, especially with toddlers, knowing that the experience of helping others is more important than a flawless outcome.

Next, look outside your home and consider how you might help others in your community. A way to start is by talking with your children about what it means to volunteer and help those in need. When your area faces a community-wide disaster—such as devastation from a tornado, hurricane, pandemic, or other crisis—be ready to offer a helping hand.

Centenarian Dr. Robert Boltan told me, "One of the most exciting times in my memory came when the hay harvest was on at the academy [school]. A beautiful hayfield along the Battle River had been obtained from which to cut acres of rich grass for the livestock. The mowing, raking, and stacking of the hay would require several days." His dad supervised the operation, and Robert and other willing students helped. Not only did the hay feed the livestock, it generated critical income to keep the school running.

No matter how big or small, children can still do amazing things to help others! As 105-year-old Anita Johnson-Mackey said, "Ask yourself, *What's the problem? What needs to be done? What can I do about it? When can I get started?*" She might have had Roman McConn of Augusta, Georgia, in mind. He was just four when he asked for

> *Volunteering is
> like knocking
> on a hidden
> door; you never
> know what
> opportunities
> might present
> themselves as
> a result.*

donations to a local animal shelter instead of birthday presents. His family had just adopted a dog from a shelter, and his mother had become a committed volunteer there. Soon they wanted to do even more. What started as a small donation to help out led to the founding of the charity organization Project Freedom Ride, which transports dogs from animal shelters with high kill rates to forever homes across the nation.[8] In addition, Roman began featuring dogs that needed new homes in brief videos, many of which went viral. In recognition of his good work, the American Society for the Prevention of Cruelty to Animals (ASPCA) named him 2018 Kid of the Year. He and Project Freedom Ride have now saved more than four thousand dogs.

Your family may also decide to lend a helping hand at the global level. Dr. Ellsworth Wareham and his wife have a fond memory of traveling to

Mexico after learning of a very sick little girl who needed heart surgery. Her family did not have the resources for or even access to the medical care she needed, but Dr. Wareham was able to go and perform lifesaving surgery. Today, child sponsorship programs from organizations like World Vision and Compassion International enable families in first world countries to provide monthly financial support so kids around the globe can get access to education, medical care, and other forms of support in their own communities. Sponsoring families receive letters from and can write to the children they support.

You might be surprised with the ideas your kids come up with as well. While sitting in his classroom, six-year-old Ryan Hreljac learned that millions of people around the world don't have safe water to drink. He went home and begged his parents to help. They offered to let Ryan raise money doing chores around the house. In a couple of months, he had earned $70 to build a well in Uganda, only to find out a well would cost over $2,000. Rather than giving up, Ryan began speaking to schools and service clubs to garner support. Wanting to do even more, in 2001 he founded Ryan's Well Foundation, which has brought drinking water to over one million people in seventeen countries.[9]

Before volunteering with your kids, be sure to ask questions so you have a good idea of what to expect. Keep in mind that volunteering doesn't mean a lengthy commitment to a particular place or person. Volunteering shouldn't be overwhelming and all-consuming; if it is, you will lose energy and incentive. Be realistic with your schedule and what will work for you. Don't feel you have to change the world. The key is to find what feels right and inspires your family to take action and make an impact.

Step 3: Connect with their why

Helping around the house and volunteering in communities should come from an internal desire to do good. God calls us to help and encourage one another. When we engage in acts of kindness, we benefit along with those we help. When it comes to assisting others, once you've connected with your *why*, you'll be more motivated to succeed.

One great reason for lending a helping hand is to gain a new sense of purpose. Want to change things up in your family in a positive way? Then volunteer. Want to stop focusing on your own worries and shift your focus to others in need? Then volunteer. Want to develop cherished family memories by doing something meaningful together? Then volunteer.

Look to donate your time to something you and your family are passionate about. The seed you plant and nurture in your children for helping others will take root and grow. Don't be surprised if this seed begins bearing fruit at a young age. It may even give your child a new sense of purpose and help direct them toward their life's calling.

One woman who began her life with nothing became world-renowned for helping the poor. This desire to help others began as a seed planted by her family during her childhood. Agnes Gonxha Bojaxhiu was born on August 26, 1910, in Skopje, Macedonia, the youngest of three children. Throughout her childhood, she was influenced by her family to take part in the church and to care about helping those in need. When she was only eight, however, her father died unexpectedly. Her mother, who often took food and clothing to the destitute and sick, became a powerful and positive influence on Agnes. She knew by age twelve that she wanted to help the poor. At eighteen,

Agnes left her family and became a missionary in India.[10] She believed that works of love are works of peace.[11] For her selfless and tremendous efforts, she was awarded the Nobel Peace Prize in 1979. We know her better by the name Mother Teresa.

Not everyone who gives as selflessly as Mother Teresa becomes famous, of course. Yet they reap many other benefits. "When you assist people," Marjorie Joseph told me, "you feel good yourself that you are making other people feel good." Marjorie—or "Sis," as she is known by her family and friends—speaks from personal experience. And Marjorie has had so much experience; at ninety-one, she's almost a centenarian. Born in Montserrat, a Caribbean island, Marjorie was one of nine children. She grew up helping her parents and her grandparents with their farm duties— from growing sweet potatoes, plantains, rice, and peas to tending to the goats, chickens, and cattle. As a teenager, Marjorie knew she wanted to help others, so she enrolled in the local nursing school. After graduation, she became one of the first public health nurses in her region. Her work was hard, strenuous, and gratifying—she helped restore many starving infants and children to full health.[12]

Though hers isn't a household name, Marjorie was honored by the queen of England herself when the governor of Montserrat presented the honor of Member of the British Empire (MBE) and the British Empire Medal to Marjorie on Elizabeth II's behalf. Marjorie has continued to help and support her local church even into her nineties. What a wonderful experience for Marjorie and for all those families she has helped.

Volunteering is like knocking on a hidden door; you never know what opportunities might present themselves as a result.

READY, SET, GO!

Now that you have seen the benefits of helping your children think of others, here are a few ideas to get you started!

Ideas for helping around the house:

- **Meal prep.** Have your children pitch in and help you with the dinnertime meal. Toddlers can help wash fruits and vegetables, while older children can cut up items and assist with directing the younger children.

- **Laundry time!** Everyone can pitch in and help with the family laundry. Older children can collect clothes and towels from around the house, place them in the washing machine, add detergent, and turn it on. Younger children can help older ones with the folding. Any of your clothes need mending? If so, encourage older children to sew up the hole—and that goes for boys, too! If a sock has a hole, place an ordinary light bulb—one you can hold in your hand—inside to stretch out the sock, making it easier to mend.

- **Scrub-a-dub.** Washing the car is especially fun in the summer for children of all ages. Kids can also help pick up items inside the car and clean up any food debris they might have dropped. Who knows—picking up after themselves a few times may make them a little tidier in the future!

- **Yard duties.** Children of all ages can help with maintaining the yard. Older children can help with mowing and weeding. Younger children can help by using safety scissors to cut back plants, raking leaves, or picking up sticks.

- **Pet care.** If you have pets like guinea pigs, rabbits, or hamsters that have cages, or a cat with a litter box, have older children clean those while younger children help watch the critter or gather cleaning supplies. Enlist your children in feeding their pets to teach them the importance of responsibility and caring for others.

Ideas for helping local and global communities:

- **Trash cleanup.** When your family takes a walk around the neighborhood, bring along a small bag to pick up any debris that needs to be thrown away or recycled.
- **Suppertime.** Invite a family over for dinner. Better yet, make it a standing invitation! Once each week or month, have them over to your home to share your meal.
- **Neighborly love.** Do elderly neighbors need help around their home? Perhaps you could pull weeds in their yard, paint their fence, help bring out their trash cans, or deliver their groceries.
- **Coins for a cause.** Raise funds and donate them for a special charity. Children are great

at coming up with ideas and implementing them. Start a lemonade stand, collect soda cans, mow yards, sell arts and crafts, or create an "-athon" event (like a walkathon, skipathon, danceathon or skateathon) or a GoFundMe page (gofundme.com) to raise money for a good cause or for someone in need. Spread the word to family, friends, and neighbors; post notices on local bulletin boards; contact newspapers or radio stations; or post online videos.

- **International support.** Join a group doing volunteer work around the globe. Your entire worldview might change after this trip of a lifetime! Check with your school or church to see if they are sponsoring any international trips. Or research organizations that organize international mission trips.[13]

CONQUERING RESISTANCE

As you begin encouraging your family to work on lending a helping hand, you may encounter a few challenges. Here are some helpful ideas to counteract some of these difficulties:

No time to volunteer. Researchers have found

that those who give away their time actually end up feeling as if they have more time than those who don't help others.[14] So pitch in and lend a hand! Don't wait for the right conditions, or you might never get started.

No place to go. Practicing the helping hand principle doesn't have to mean leaving your community. All you need is a different perspective. Why not invite over neighbors, family, or friends—especially those going through a hard time—to enjoy a movie or game night? Or your family could raise funds for a cause you're interested in and donate the money.

No luck on first try. If you decide a volunteer assignment wasn't a great fit, try another. Be sure to look for environments or events your family is interested in. If you enjoy spending time in nature, find a way to volunteer in the outdoors. If your family enjoys singing or playing instruments, incorporate your musical talents in your outreach (like performing at a nursing home).

Nothing to offer. Don't assume you don't have needed skills or talents. Take the initiative to offer someone a helping hand or an encouraging word. Create your own Meetup group (Meetup.com) to meet other families in your community who want to pool their talents and help each other or another local group. Or post on Nextdoor (nextdoor.com), a website geared to keep members of local communities informed and connected.

If you want to grow your village, lending a helping hand is a great way to increase and strengthen your connections.

In Conclusion ...

Keep going!

CENTENARIAN SALMA MOHR

THE WINTER'S DAY WHEN I SAT ON our patio watching Julia dig in the dirt seems so long ago—as does my family's harried, junk-food-fueled life. It hasn't always been easy, and we still have a lot of work to do, but my family and I have benefitted tremendously from this journey. We are more aware of the impact our daily choices have on our overall health, happiness, and ability to thrive in the face of adversity.

I measure my family's progress in several ways: Cholesterol is down, weight is down, headaches are fewer, happiness is up (though sibling rivalry is still a common theme), communication is better, my children's initiative is slightly up, our pace of life is slowing, and our contentment is growing.

The other day, I went to visit centenarian Salma Mohr. After I updated her on my family, she told me, "You're getting it! Keep going!" As a retired teacher, she couldn't help but assign me a grade, which I'm happy to report was an A. Then she asked, "Are you using the knitted cloth I gave you to clean your kitchen?" Almost one hundred years ago, when her siblings did housekeeping to provide for their family and put Salma through college, they thought she might never learn to clean well. Now she is teaching and inspiring so many, not only to clean our kitchens but to clean up our lives.

"Thank you so much, Salma, for teaching me a better way!" I whispered to her as Julia and I gave her an affectionate hug before packing up to leave. I am grateful for the many centenarians who shared their wisdom, which I've been able to put into practice with my own family.

Setbacks have occurred—like the time my son crushed his nose during a school basketball game. In the middle of that crisis, our habit #3 was flung aside while fast food flew in. (There's a reason the Golden Arches are located near hospitals.)

Challenges will occur. Life happens. But unexpected difficulties can make you stronger and help you rely on some of these new habits even more. Some days I do better than others, but I'm in it for the long haul and I hope you will be too!

Leave your inherent pursuit of perfection at the door and step inside and connect, because when you invest time and energy in developing these habits, you give yourself and your family a gift, one with both immediate and long-lasting benefits. In addition to better health, you are likely to see an increase in your children's happiness and their ability to perform at all their endeavors, including school, work, sports, music, and much more.

I have tried to give you a few ideas to get started, but I encourage you to use your own resources and ingenuity to come up with family-specific strategies that work for you. Be nimble and adaptable. Fortify yourself for future setbacks by always keeping your eyes on the goal. As a parent, you are in the seed-planting business, laying the groundwork for health, happiness, and even higher performance. Remember, big things often have small beginnings.

This is the bigger story that you are creating, connecting with a previous generation to discover their secrets and carrying those lessons forward in your generation and those to come.

Ready?

Set?

Go!

NOTES

INTRODUCTION: ONE-HUNDRED-YEAR-OLD WISDOM

1. "History of Blue Zones," Blue Zones website, accessed October 29, 2020, https://www.bluezones.com/about /history/.
2. The quotes from these interviews in the book are as close as possible to the transcripts. In some instances, a word was added or a slight change made to ensure readers better understand what was being reported.

HABITS #1 AND #2: ACTIVE MOVEMENT AND OUTDOOR ENGAGEMENT

1. Press Association, "Children Spend Only Half As Much Time Playing Outside As Their Parents Did," *The Guardian*, July 27, 2016, https://www.theguardian.com /environment/2016/jul/27/children-spend-only-half -the-time-playing-outside-as-their-parents-did.
2. Danielle Cohen, "Why Kids Need to Spend Time in Nature," Child Mind Institute, https://childmind.org /article/why-kids-need-to-spend-time-in-nature/.
3. Richard Louv, *Last Child in the Woods: Saving Our Children from Nature-Deficit Disorder* (Chapel Hill, NC: Algonquin Books, 2008).
4. For information on Robbie Bond and Kids Speak for Parks, visit https://www.kidsspeakforparks.org/. Accessed March 21, 2020.

HABIT #3: EAT SIMPLY

1. Marcos Paseggi, "It Is Possible to Be a Very Unhealthy Vegetarian," *Adventist Review*, March 1, 2018, https://www.adventistreview.org/church-news/story 5903-it-is-possible-to-be-a-very-unhealthy-vegetarian.

2. "Choose My Plate," US Department of Agriculture (USDA), accessed March 21, 2020, https://www.choosemyplate.gov/.

3. "The Water in You: Water and the Human Body," US Geological Survey (USGS), US Department of the Interior, accessed March 4, 2020, https://www.usgs.gov/special-topic/water-science-school/science/water-you-water-and-human-body?qt-science_center_objects=0#qt-science_center_objects.

4. Erica L. Kenney et al., "Prevalence of Inadequate Hydration among US Children and Disparities by Gender and Race/Ethnicity: National Health and Nutrition Examination Survey, 2009–2012," *American Journal of Public Health* 105, no. 8 (August 2015): e113–18, https://doi.org/10.2105/AJPH.2015.302572. See also, Kory Taylor and Elizabeth B. Jones, "Adult Dehydration" in *StatPearls* (Treasure Island, FL: StatPearls Publishing, 2022), https://www.ncbi.nlm.nih.gov/books/NBK555956/.

5. "2020–2025 Make Every Bite Count with the Dietary Guidelines," Dietary Guidelines for Americans (DGA), accessed June 27, 2022, https://www.dietaryguidelines.gov/sites/default/files/2021-03/Dietary_Guidelines_for_Americans-2020-2025.pdf.

HABIT #4: REST AND RESET

1. University of Chicago Medical Center, "New Study Shows People Sleep Even Less than They Think," ScienceDaily, July 3, 2006, www.sciencedaily.com/releases/2006/07/060703162945.htm.

2. Jeffrey M. Jones, "In US, 40% Get Less than Recommended Amount of Sleep," Gallup News, December 19, 2013, https://news.gallup.com/poll/166553/less-recommended-amount-sleep.aspx.

3. Neil Howe, "America the Sleep-Deprived," *Forbes*, August 18, 2017, https://www.forbes.com/sites/neilhowe/2017/08/18/america-the-sleep-deprived/#470eb89e1a38.

4. "Paid Time Off Trends in the US," US Travel Association, accessed March 21, 2020, https://www.ustravel.org/sites/default/files/media_root/document/Paid%20Time%20Off%20Trends%20Fact%20Sheet.pdf.

5. Michikazu Sekine et al., "A Dose-Response Relationship between Short Sleeping Hours and Childhood Obesity: Results of the Toyama Birth Cohort Study," *Child: Care, Health and Development* 28, no. 2 (April 20, 2002): 163–70, https://doi.org/10.1046/j.1365-2214.2002.00260.x.

6. Alicja R. Rudnicka et al., "Sleep Duration and Risk of Type 2 Diabetes," *Pediatrics* 140, no. 3 (September 2017): e20170338, https://doi.org/10.1542/peds.2017-0338.

7. Elsie M. Taveras et al., "Prospective Study of Insufficient Sleep and Neurobehavioral Functioning among School-Age Children," *Academic Pediatrics* 17, no. 6 (August 2017): 625–32, https://doi.org/10.1016/j.acap.2017.02.001.

8. Anna S. Urrila et al., "Sleep Habits, Academic Performance, and the Adolescent Brain Structure," *Scientific Reports* (February 9, 2017): 7, https://doi.org/10.1038/srep41678.

9. Lisa Rapaport, "Strict Bedtime Rules Can Help Kids Get Enough Sleep," Reuters, June 1, 2017, https://www.reuters.com/article/us-health-parenting-child

-sleep/strict-bedtime-rules-can-help-kids-get-enough
-sleep-idUSKBN18S6F8.

10. Stephen King, *On Writing: A Memoir of the Craft* (New York: Scribner; 2000), 165.

11. Jianghong Liu et al., "Midday Napping in Children: Associations between Nap Frequency and Duration across Cognitive, Positive Psychological Well-Being, Behavioral, and Metabolic Health Outcomes," *Sleep* 42, no. 9 (September 6, 2019): zsz126, https://doi.org/10.1093/sleep/zsz126.

12. Danielle Pacheco, "The Best Temperature for Sleep," SleepFoundation.org, last updated March 11, 2022, https://www.sleepfoundation.org/bedroom -environment/best-temperature-for-sleep.

HABIT #5: CULTIVATE LIFE-GIVING RELATIONSHIPS

1. Katharine Gammon, "Penguins: The Math behind the Huddle," *Inside Science*, an editorially independent news service of the American Institute of Physics, November 20, 2012, https://insidescience.org/news /penguins-math-behind-huddle.

2. Robyn Fivush, Marshall Duke, and Jennifer G. Bohanek, "'Do You Know . . .': The Power of Family History in Adolescent Identity and Well-Being," *Journal of Family Life* (February 23, 2010), https:// ncph.org/wp-content/uploads/2013/12/The-power -of-family-history-in-adolescent-identity.pdf.

3. Luke 10:30-37.

HABIT #6: BUILD A FOUNDATION OF FAITH

1. Mohd Ahsan Kabir Rizvi and Mohammad Zakir Hossain, "Relationship between Religious Belief and Happiness: A Systematic Literature Review," *Journal of Religion and Health* 56, no. 5 (October 2017): 1561–82, https://doi.org/10.1007/s10943-016-0332-6.

2. Stuart R. Varon and Anne W. Riley, "Relationship between Maternal Church Attendance and Adolescent Mental Health and Social Functioning," *Psychiatric Services* 50, no. 6 (June 1999): 799–805, https://doi.org/10.1176/ps.50.6.799.

3. James W. Anderson and Paige A. Nunnelley, "Private Prayer Associations with Depression, Anxiety, and Other Health Conditions: An Analytical Review of Clinical Studies," *Postgraduate Medicine* 128, no. 7 (September 2016): 635–41, https://doi.org/10.1080/00325481.2016.1209962.

4. Connie Svob et al., "Association of Parent and Offspring Religiosity with Offspring Suicide Ideation and Attempts," *JAMA Psychiatry* 75, no. 10 (October 1, 2018): 1062–70, https://doi.org/10.1001/jamapsychiatry.2018.2060.

5. Shanshan Li et al., "Association of Religious Service Attendance with Mortality among Women," *JAMA Internal Medicine* 176, no. 6 (June 1, 2016): 777–85, https://doi.org/10.1001/jamainternmed.2016.1615.

6. Tyler J. VanderWeele et al., "Association between Religious Service Attendance and Lower Suicide Rates among US Women," *JAMA Psychiatry* 73, no. 8 (August 1, 2016): 845–51, https://doi.org/10.1001/jamapsychiatry.2016.1243.

7. Christopher P. Salas-Wright et al., "Religiosity Profiles of American Youth in Relation to Substance Use, Violence, and Delinquency," *Journal of Youth and Adolescence* 41, no. 12 (December 2012): 1560–75, https://doi.org/10.1007/s10964-012-9761-z.

8. Ronald F. Inglehart, "Giving Up on God: The Global Decline of Religion," *Foreign Affairs*, September/October 2020, 110–18, https://www.foreignaffairs.com/articles/world/2020-08-11/religion-giving-god.

9. Gabe Bullard, "The World's Newest Major Religion: No Religion," *National Geographic*, April 22, 2016, https://www.nationalgeographic.com/news/2016

/04/160422-atheism-agnostic-secular-nones-rising
-religion/.

10. Claire Gecewicz, "Few Americans Say Their House
of Worship Is Open, but a Quarter Say Their Faith
Has Grown amid Pandemic," Pew Research Center,
April 30, 2020, https://www.pewresearch.org/fact
-tank/2020/04/30/few-americans-say-their-house
-of-worship-is-open-but-a-quarter-say-their-religious
-faith-has-grown-amid-pandemic/.

11. Harold G. Koenig, "Religion, Spirituality, and
Health: The Research and Clinical Implications,"
International Scholarly Research Notices Psychiatry
(2012): 278730, https://www.ncbi.nlm.nih.gov
/pmc/articles/PMC3671693/; Laura B. Koenig and
George E. Vaillant, "A Prospective Study of Church
Attendance and Health over the Lifespan," *Health
Psychology* 28, no. 1 (January 2009): 117–24,
https://doi.org/10.1037/a0012984.

12. Marcie C. Goeke-Morey et al., "Maternal Religiosity,
Family Resources and Stressors, and Parent-Child
Attachment Security in Northern Ireland," *Social
Development* 22, no. 1 (February 2013):
19–37, https://doi.org/10.1111/j.1467-9507
.2012.00659.x.

13. Başak Çoruh et al., "Does Religious Activity Improve
Health Outcomes? A Critical Review of the Recent
Literature," *Explore* 1, no. 3 (May 2005): 186–91,
https://doi.org/10.1016/j.explore.2005.02.001.

14. Camila Csizmar Carvalho et al., "Effectiveness of Prayer
in Reducing Anxiety in Cancer Patients," *Revista da
Escola de Enfermagem da U S P* 48, no. 4 (August 2014):
683–89, https://pubmed.ncbi.nlm.nih.gov/25338250/;
Peter A. Boelens et al., "A Randomized Trial of the Effect
of Prayer on Depression and Anxiety," *International
Journal of Psychiatry in Medicine* 39, no. 4 (2009):
377–92, https://doi.org/10.2190/PM.39.4.c.

HABIT #7: DEVELOP A POSITIVE MINDSET

1. Nadja Walter, Lucie Nikoleizig, and Dorothee Alfermann, "Effects of Self-Talk Training on Competitive Anxiety, Self-Efficacy, Volitional Skills, and Performance: An Intervention Study with Junior Sub-Elite Athletes," *Sports* (Basel, Switzerland) 7, no. 6 (June 2019): 148, https://doi.org/10.3390/sports7060148.

2. See Nick Vujicic's website Life without Limbs, accessed April 5, 2020, https://www.lifewithoutlimbs.org/.

3. Boris Vujicic, "My Son Was Born with No Arms or Legs and It's Nothing Like You're Thinking," *Fatherly*, July 29, 2016, https://www.fatherly.com/health -science/nick-vujicics-father-on-raising-a-boy-with -no-arms-or-legs/.

4. Rosie Perper, "Photos and Charts Show How the Natural World Is Thriving Now That Humans Are Staying Indoors," *Insider*, April 22, 2020, https:// www.insider.com/photos-videos-earth-planet-thriving -coronavirus-2020-4.

5. Robert A. Emmons and Michael E. McCullough, "Counting Blessings versus Burdens: An Experimental Investigation of Gratitude and Subjective Well-Being in Daily Life," *Journal of Personality and Social Psychology* 84, no. 2 (February 2003): 377–89, https://doi.org /10.1037/0022-3514.84.2.377.

6. Izabela Krejtz et al., "Counting One's Blessings Can Reduce the Impact of Daily Stress," *Journal of Happiness Studies* 17 (2016): 25–39, https://doi.org/10.1007 /s10902-014-9578-4.

HABIT #8: HELP OTHERS

1. "60 Minutes Presents: Amazing Kids," *60 Minutes*, CBS News, February 2, 2014, https://www.cbsnews .com/news/60-minutes-presents-amazing-kids/.

2. Leanne Arsenault, "Research on Household Chores," *Raising Strong Girls* podcast, Society for the Psychology

of Women, July 2017, https://www.apadivisions
.org/division-35/news-events/news/household
-chores.

3. "Should You Make Your Child Do Chores? Majority
of Kids 'Get Away with NO Cleaning,'" *Express*,
October 25, 2017, https://www.express.co.uk/life
-style/life/870542/children-chores-majority-kids-no
-cleaning-parents; Marc Montgomery, "Children and
Household Chores: Developing Life Skills," Radio
Canada International, March 30, 2016, https://www
.rcinet.ca/en/2016/03/30/children-and-household
-chores-developing-life-skills/; Shi Li, "'It's All about
Me, Me, Me!' Why Children Are Spending Less
Time Doing Household Chores," The Conversation,
October 6, 2016, https://theconversation.com/its
-all-about-me-me-me-why-children-are-spending
-less-time-doing-household-chores-66134.

4. Richard Rende and Jen Prosek, *Raising Can-Do Kids:
Giving Children the Tools to Thrive in a Fast-Changing
World* (New York: TarcherPerigee, 2015).

5. Barbara Rogoff, "Learning by Observing and Pitching
In to Family and Community Endeavors: An
Orientation," *Human Development* 57, no. 2 (2014):
69–81, https://www.jstor.org/stable/26764709.

6. Richard M. Sherman and Robert B. Sherman,
"A Spoonful of Sugar," from *Mary Poppins Original
Soundtrack*, Walt Disney Records, 1964.

7. "Responsibility and Chores: Part 1—Benefits of
Chores," The Center for Parenting Education, accessed
April 10, 2020, https://centerforparentingeducation
.org/library-of-articles/responsibility-and-chores/part
-i-benefits-of-chores/.

8. For more about Roman McConn and Project Freedom
Ride, see their website at http://projectfreedomride
.org/; "Meet the 7-Year-Old Boy Who Has Rescued

More than 1,000 Dogs from Kill Shelters," *Inside Edition*, July 13, 2018, https://www.insideedition.com/meet-7-year-old-boy-who-has-rescued-more-1000-dogs-kill-shelters-44973.

9. Ryan Hreljac, "Ryan's Story," Ryan's Well Foundation, https://www.ryanswell.ca/about-ryans-well/ryans-story; for an overview of the foundation's work, see https://www.ryanswell.ca/.

10. Kathryn Spink, *Mother Teresa: A Complete Authorized Biography* (New York: HarperCollins, 1997), 6–12.

11. See Michael Collopy, *Works of Love Are Works of Peace* (San Francisco: Ignatius Press, 1996).

12. Marjorie Joseph tells her story in her autobiography, *God Has Brought Me This Far* (Fort Oglethorpe, GA: TEACH Services, 2007).

13. One such group I'm familiar with is Maranatha Volunteers International. Learn more at https://maranatha.org.

14. Cassie Mogilner, Zoë Chance, and Michael I. Norton, "Giving Time Gives You Time," *Psychological Science* 23, no. 10 (September 12, 2012): 1233–38, https://doi.org/10.1177/0956797612442551; Cassie Mogilner, "You'll Feel Less Rushed If You Give Time Away," *Harvard Business Review*, September 1, 2012, https://hbr.org/2012/09/youll-feel-less-rushed-if-you-give-time-away.

ABOUT THE AUTHOR

RHONDA SPENCER-HWANG, who holds a doctorate in public health, is an epidemiologist, an associate professor in the School of Public Health at Loma Linda University, and a member of the world's first identified Resiliency Capital, a Christian community known for its healthy lifestyles. Dr. Spencer-Hwang's groundbreaking research on centenarians offers a unique perspective on developing whole health and resilience, which are especially important for families today. Despite adverse childhood experiences (ACEs) and stressors faced throughout their lifetime, from pandemics to pollution and economic recession, these centenarians offer valuable insights on healthy living.

With more than twenty-five years of experience in public health, Dr. Spencer-Hwang has appeared in multiple international documentaries discussing her findings and lifestyle practices, has written for numerous peer-reviewed publications, has given presentations around the world, and has stewarded funding from various government agencies as she promotes resiliency and a culture of health, especially for children. She is an expert at using art and play to promote health in both children and adults. Furthermore, Dr. Spencer-Hwang has worked the front lines as an epidemiologist combating the spread of infectious disease. Now through her research-based Resiliency Program, she helps children and adults develop healthy and resilient lifestyles to withstand whatever life throws their way.

Dr. Spencer-Hwang and her husband enjoy raising their children, Jayden, Joelle, and Julia, in Loma Linda, California.